CREATING
DATA-DRIVEN
WEBSITES

CREATING DATA-DRIVEN WEBSITES

AN INTRODUCTION TO HTML, CSS, PHP, AND MYSQL

BOB TERRELL

MOMENTUM PRESS
ENGINEERING

Creating Data-Driven Websites: An Introduction to HTML, CSS, PHP, and MySQL

First published by Momentum Press®, LLC
222 East 46th Street, New York, NY 10017
www.momentumpress.net

ISBN-13: 978-1-94664-604-0 (print)
ISBN-13: 978-1-94664-605-7 (e-book)

Momentum Press Computer Science Collection

Cover and interior design by S4Carlisle Publishing Services Private Ltd., Chennai, India

10 9 8 7 6 5 4 3 2 1

Printed in the United States of America

ABSTRACT

Today's modern world is heavily dependent on the World Wide Web. It affects the way we communicate, how we shop, and how we learn about the world. Every website, every page, consists of four fundamental elements: the structure, the style, the programming, and the data. These correspond to four different "languages," respectively: HTML, CSS, PHP, and MySQL.

The purpose of this book is to provide an introduction to this set of technologies to teach a new programmer how to get started creating data-driven websites and to provide a jumping-off point for the reader to expand his or her skills. After learning the necessary components, users will have the understanding required to use the above technologies to create a working website. This book is aimed at the programmer or student who understands the basic building blocks of programming such as statements and control structures but lacks knowledge of the syntax and application of the above-mentioned technologies.

KEYWORDS

HTML; PHP; website; MAMP; LAMP; databases; CSS; structured query language; SQL; MySQL

CONTENTS

ACKNOWLEDGMENTS

I would like to thank my wife for her patience and understanding and for occupying the time of three children long enough to write this book; Lisa MacLean, for being my favorite professor; my parents, for always seeing the potential in me and wanting the best for me; and fate, for life has given me many blessings and opportunities arising from circumstances that reach far beyond my own actions.

INTRODUCTION

The purpose of this book is to teach you, the reader, the basics of web development. Web development is made up of many different parts and uses many different languages. The languages that this book uses are HTML, CSS, PHP, and MySQL. These languages, and the software to interpret them, are freely available and can run on Windows, macOS, and Linux, making them a natural choice for the beginner.

PROJECT

As an example, through the course of this book, we will create a fully functioning project: a style guide. When multiple programmers work on a project together, it's common for them to have learned multiple different customs when coding. It isn't generally important whether a line is indented with four spaces or a tab, but it is important that the same method be used consistently throughout code. In a more general sense, this can be thought of as a suggestion box. Users (in this case, our hypothetical fellow coders) make suggestions regarding the style to be used a collaborative project, and the group as a whole votes on them. Those suggestions that receive majority approval are considered to be part of the guide.

When designing a site, it helps to think about the various tasks it will need to perform. Generally speaking, each task will be a separate script (or page). Just from our description, we have a short list of tasks that the site must perform:

1. Accept a suggestion from a user.
2. Allow users to vote on suggestions.
3. Determine whether a suggestion has a majority vote.
4. Display approved suggestions together.

This, however, is overly general. Each of these involves several smaller tasks. We also need an index (landing) page, something to show users who first visit the site. A more detailed, structured list would look as follows:

a. Index page. As a landing page, it should do the following:
 1. Have a link to approved suggestions (the guide).
 2. Contain a login link so we can distinguish between the different users and track their votes.

b. Handle users. As the administrator, we can create a section to handle user-related tasks. Specific tasks in this section should do the following:
 1. Display the list of users.
 2. Delete a user who is no longer with us.

c. Handle suggestions.
 1. Allow users to create a suggestion.
 2. Display a list of suggestions.
 3. Display details about a particular suggestion.
 4. Allow users to comment on a suggestion before voting, in case clarification is needed.
 5. Allow users to vote on a suggestion.

We may find as we proceed that even this isn't quite detailed enough, but it will be sufficient for now.

BEFORE WE BEGIN...

As part of the project in this book, you will need a host with PHP, MySQL, and your choice of web server software. Apache is common on Mac and Linux; Windows users may use IIS (Internet Information Services). The host need not be from a web services provider; your personal computer is sufficient to run all of these. If you do not have a host set up for you, search for a guide to help you install these software packages on your machine.

CHAPTER 1

HTML

HTML is not, strictly, a programming language. HTML stands for hyper-text markup language. It is a way of marking text, so that a web browser knows how to display it. It can be considered the most basic "building block" of a web page, and as such, it is where we begin.

It is customary when teaching a new language to begin with a simple program that simply outputs *Hello, world!* With HTML, it couldn't be simpler. Open a new document in your editor and type in "Hello, world!", as seen below (Figure 1.1).

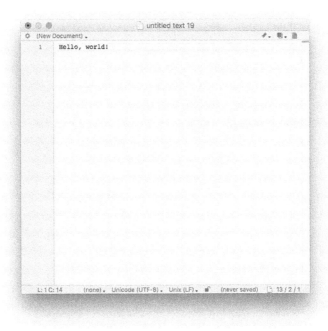

Figure 1.1. Desc: "Hello, world!" in a text editor window

Save the file to your web root with the name *hi.html* (Figure 1.2).

Figure 1.2. Desc: file "hi.html" visible in a folder

View the results in your web browser of choice. Enter in the URL for your web root, and add *hi.html* to the end (Figure 1.3).
You're done!

Figure 1.3. Desc: "Hello, world!" displayed in a web browser

FUNDAMENTALS

So what's really going on here? The short answer is *it is the browser's job to make as much sense of an HTML file as it can.* We can see what it has done by inspecting the web page. In Chrome: *View -> Developer -> Developer Tools.* In the window or pane that opens, select the *Elements* tab. We see that the browser has taken our file, which the web server has told it is an HTML file (thanks to the *.html* extension) and added to it. We should see something like the following (Figure 1.4):

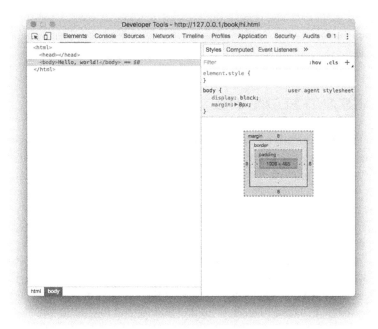

Figure 1.4. Developer Tools window in Chrome

The document is located on the left. We see our *Hello, world!* text on the left. What's the rest of that?

An HTML file is rendered by the browser into a document with *elements.* Note the three elements in document: the *<html>* element, which encompasses the entire document; the *<head>* element, which is currently empty and provides information about the document; and the *<body>* element, which contains the part of the document that the web browser is intended to render. Because our file contained only plain text, the browser created enough elements for our document to make sense. It put the contents of our file into the <body> element.

Revisit the document in the text editor and add in some of the elements the browser filled in on its own. Change the document to be as such:

```
<html>
<head></head>
<body>Hello, world!</body>
</html>
```

Save the file and refresh the browser window. It should look pretty much the same! Only this time, the browser is reading our file and *parsing* (making sense of) it.

TAGS AND ELEMENTS

An html file is made up of markup contained in *tags*. An HTML *tag* consists of an open angle bracket (less than sign), certain characters to denote the type of tag, and a closing angle bracket (greater than sign). Tags may not have a space between the opening angle bracket and the letters. In the file above, note that we have three tags: <html>, <head>, and <body>. These correspond to the html, head, and body elements that the browser renders in its document.

HTML tags usually come in sets. There is an *opening tag*, as described above, and there is a *closing tag*, telling the browser when the element in question should end. A closing tag is an angle bracket, followed by a slash, followed by the same characters used in the opening tag. In the file above, every opening tag has a corresponding closing tag. A more correct description of our file would be that there are three opening tags: <html>, <head>, and <body>; and three closing tags: </head>, </body>, and </html>.

Also note that HTML is hierarchical: Elements can contain other elements when tags of another element are found in between the opening and closing tags. The *head* and *body* elements are contained within the *html* element because the <head> and <body> tags appear between the opening <html> and closing </html> tags.

While it's possible to not close tags—if our file above was missing the closing tags, the browser would still render it correctly—some tags must be closed, and the browser will always try to render a document as if it were well-formed. It's also possible to close tags not in reverse order: For example, the following would most likely render correctly:

```
<p>This is some <b><u>important</b></u>
   text.
```

but it is not well-formed. The following is well-formed:

```
<p>This is some <b><u>important</u></b>
   text.</p>
```

Note the differences. The `</u>` closing tag closes the `<u>` element, which was the last one opened, followed by `</b>` to end the `<b>` opening tag. We also properly closed the `<p>` tag with the closing `</p>` tag. Don't worry if you aren't familiar with what these tags do! They'll be explained soon enough. For now, simply note what it means to have well-formed HTML: that tags are closed in reverse order that they are opened.

BEST PRACTICE

Although web browsers give their best effort to make sense of an HTML file, throughout this book we will endeavor to generate *well-formed* documents. A well-formed document is one which always closes HTML tags and closes them in the reverse of the order opened. HTML documents that follow this guideline are easier for humans to read and understand, and following this practice makes it harder to make a mistake in which the web browser becomes legitimately confused.

ATTRIBUTES AND PROPERTIES

The HTML tags covered so far are tags at their most basic. They open an element, and they close an element. Tags, however, can also have *attributes*, which define an element's *properties*. (Sometimes, properties can be changed on an HTML document. To be more precise, attributes define an element's initial properties.) The attributes that can be used in a tag vary depending upon the tag type, but nearly every html tag can contain the attributes *id* and *class*. Consider the following:

```
<p id="myId" class="myClass">This is some
   <b><u>important</u></b> text.</p>
```

In the code above, we've added the *id* attribute, with the value *myId*, and the *class* attribute, with the value *myClass*. These become properties of the rendered *p* element. The *id* and *class* attributes don't do anything on their own, but we'll be revisiting them later.

BLOCK ELEMENTS

HTML elements are considered either *block* elements or *inline* elements. Block elements begin a new line, and they usually try to be as wide as possible. The following is a list of the most common block-level elements:

- **p**: short for **paragraph**. This is used to contain a paragraph of text. Multiple paragraphs will have space between them
- **h1, h2, h3, h4, h5,** and **h6** : These six elements are all **header** elements. They are intended to be used hierarchically; the main header is **h1**, the first subheader is **h2**, the next level down is **h3**, and so forth.
- **ol, ul, li**: short for **ordered list** and **unordered list**. They contain **li** elements, which are **list items**. An ordered list will number the items. An unordered list will use bullet marks.
- **hr**: Short for **horizontal rule**, this is used to denote a break by drawing a line across the document.
- **pre**: This element contains **preformatted text**. Any text within this element will be displayed in a monospace font and with any line breaks left intact.
- **table**: The **table** element is used to display tabular data. It will consist of table rows (**tr**), which in turn contain table data cells (**td**) or table headers (**th**). The **td** and **th** elements contain one attribute worth mentioning here: *colspan*, which specifies how many columns the element should span.
- **div**: The **div** element is a generic block-level element. Think of it as a "page division." They have no particular behavior on their own, but are often used with Cascading Style Sheets (CSS) to position elements in a certain way.

Let's take a moment to practice using these elements. Put the following in a document.

```
<html>
<head></head>
<body>
<p>This text is inside a paragraph tag.
```

```
It's worth noting that,
in HTML, we can have line breaks
wherever we want, but the browser will ignore
    them.</p>
<pre>On the other hand,
preformatted text preserves white space.</pre>
<p>A simple multiplication table:</p>
<table>
<tr><td></td><th>1</th><th>2</th>
    <th>3</th><th>4</th></tr>
<tr><th>1</th><td>1</td><td>2</td>
    <td>3</td><td>4</td></tr>
<tr><th>2</th><td>2</td><td>4</td>
    <td>6</td><td>8</td></tr>
<tr><th>3</th><td>3</td><td>6</td>
    <td>9</td><td>12</td></tr>
<tr><th>4</th><td>4</td><td>8</td>
    <td>12</td><td>16</td></tr>
</table>
<p>Our shopping list:</p>
<ul>
<li>Bread</li>
<li>Milk</li>
<li>Eggs</li>
</ul>
<p>Our to do list:</p>
<ol>
<li>Drop off dry cleaning</li>
<li>Pick up Tim from school.</li>
<li>Drop Jan off at soccer practice.</li>
</ol>
</body>
</html>
```

How does the HTML above appear in your browser?

INLINE ELEMENTS

Unlike block elements, inline elements do not create a new line. They exist within the flow of the content around them. Inline elements should not contain block elements, but may contain other inline elements. Most inline elements make use of their attributes to help define their behavior. The following are the most common inline elements:

- **b, i, u**: These elements simply make the text inside them bold, italic, or underlined, respectively. It's often easier and better to use CSS for this (more later), though there's no harm in using these to italicize a book title, for example.
- **em, strong**: Short for emphasis and strong. These elements behave much like **i** and **b**, respectively, with the added bonus that text-to-speech screen readers will read them differently. Whenever you want to draw attention to words, you should prefer these elements to simply making the text bold or italic.
- **a**: Short for anchor tag. This tag is used to generate links to other documents. Its notable attribute is *href*, the value of which is the path on the server to the other document, relative to the current one. An absolute path may also be used if linking to another site.
- **img**: This is the image tag, used to include an image in your document. **img** typically uses the following attributes: *src* specifies the source of the image. Much like the **a** tag, this is the path to the image file, relative to the current document, or an absolute path if including an image from elsewhere. *alt* specifies alternative text to display if the image can't be displayed. *height* and *width* are both optional. If used, they are the height and width the image will be displayed, in pixels.
- **span**: This is the inline equivalent of **div**. It does nothing on its own, but it can be used to mark off a section of the document to be used by something else, such as CSS.

FORM ELEMENTS

In the earliest days of the Internet, websites were simply pages up for display. You read them, you clicked around, and you went on your merry way. That's hardly the case nowadays, and HTML forms are a big reason why. Forms allow data to be sent to the server to be processed. Forms can be used for search fields, or for registering at a site. Any time a site submits user-provided data back to the server, it's likely to be using a form. On to the form elements:

- **form**: The **form** element itself is a block element. It contains many other elements that together allow users to enter data. **form** has two main attributes: *action*, which specifies the document that will handle the form; and *method*, which is how the information will be sent. Note that while **form** is a block element, most elements it contains are inline elements.

- **input**: Used to specify input as part of a **form**. The **input** element does a lot of work, depending on its attributes. All of the following are attributes of the **input** element:
  - *type*: The most important attribute, this is the type of input we want. Valid values most commonly used are ***checkbox***, for a simple checkbox; ***radio***, for linked buttons that allow only one to be chosen; ***text***, which presents a single-line text field; ***password***, which acts much like ***text***, except that anything entered is obscured by the browser; and ***hidden***, which is not displayed to the user.
  - *checked*: The *checked* attribute specifies whether an input of *type* ***checkbox*** or ***radio*** should be displayed as already checked. The mere presence of this attribute means it should, so any value is unneeded, but often it is assigned a value of "yes" or "checked".
  - *disabled*: A *disabled* form element is one that is displayed but cannot be interacted with or changed. Notably, any disabled form elements are **NOT** sent when the form is submitted.
  - *name*: This is the name the form element will have when processed.
  - *value*: An initial value for the form element may be set with this attribute.
- **label**: A **label** is used together with **input** elements to allow the user to click on the text label as if they were clicking on the input element itself. This is especially useful for ***checkbox*** and ***radio*** buttons.
- **select**: The **select** element allows the user to choose from a list of predefined **option**s. When using the **select** element, the *name* attribute is placed on the **select** element, whereas each **option** element may have its own *value* attribute. If it is not used, the default value of an **option** is the text contained inside it.
- **textarea**: The **textarea** element is simply a multiline text input. You can use the *rows* and *cols* attributes to specify the number of text rows and columns (roughly, characters) it should take up.

ENTITIES

One last topic of note in the world of HTML is *entities*. Recall that HTML tags are the < symbol, followed by a tag name, and any attributes are part of the tag until the closing $>$ character. This seems pretty straightforward, but what if we need a web page to say the following?

```
if a<b and b<c, then a<c
```

At first glance, the problem may not be apparent, but put that in a document and view it in a browser. All we see is *if a*. What happened? Well, the $<b$ and everything after it was treated as a tag. That's not what we wanted! Thankfully, HTML provides us with a way to output special HTML characters without having them treated as tags: entities. The six most common entities are listed in the table below:

Character	Description	Entity
<	Less than	&lt;
>	Greater than	&gt;
"	Quotation mark	&quot;
'	Apostrophe (or single quote)	&apos;
&	Ampersand	&amp;
	nonbreaking space	

The non-breaking space is exactly what it sounds like: A space between two words that doesn't allow a line break. It's not necessary to use an entity absolutely everywhere; for example, in normal text, a quotation mark won't be confused as anything else. However, if you must include a quotation mark inside a quoted attribute value, an entity would be required. Below are some examples:

```
if a&lt;b and b&lt;c, then a&lt;c<br/>
if a&lt;b and b&gt;c, it is unknown whether
    a&lt;c or a&gt;c

<option value='Fermat&apos;s Last Theorem'>
    Fermat's Last Theorem</option>
<option value="She said, &quot;Hello.&quot;">
    She said, "Hello."</option>
```

It's also possible to encode a reserved HTML character (and in fact, *any* character) as an entity using the character's decimal ASCII (or even Unicode) character number. &, for example, has a character code of

38 and can therefore be replaced by either *&* or *&*. Likewise, it is possible—though pointless—to use *A* instead of the letter *A*. Although using named entities is generally preferred, as it's clearer what the character will be, the numeric version is also allowed.

COMMENTS

Comments may be used inside HTML. A comment begins with the string *<!--* and ends with *-->*. It may span multiple lines if necessary. HTML comments are sent to the browser, but the browser ignores their contents. However, because they are sent to the browser, they aren't used very often; comments are for *you*, not for the users of your site. Nevertheless, if there's a "secret" message you want to send to your users, an HTML comment would be a fun place to put it.

```
<!-- I'm learning HTML! -->
```

The above would appear when a user viewed the source of your web page, but it wouldn't appear on the page when the browser renders it.

PROJECT

As much of our project involves dynamically generated content, there isn't much we can accomplish yet. There are, however, a couple of tasks we can at least begin. We can create pages for the form to input a new user and the form to add a suggestion. We can also create an index page to link to these forms. As that describes three tasks, we will be creating three files.

Let's begin with adding users. Each piece of information we want to store should be its own field. About our users, we need to store a username and password, so they can log in. We might also want to store their first name, last name, and job title within our fictional company. Put the below HTML into a file named *user-new.html*:

```
<html>
<head>
<title>Add User</title>
</head>
```

```html
<body>
<p>Please add a new user below.</p>
<form action="user-save.php" method="post">
<p>Username: <input type="text" name=
    "name" /></p>
<p>Password: <input type="text" name=
    "pass" /></p>
<p>First Name: <input type="text" name=
    "first" /></p>
<p>Last Name: <input type="text" name=
    "last" /></p>
<p>Title: <input type="text" name=
    "title" /></p>
<p><input type="submit" name="action"
    value="Save" /> <input type="submit"
    name="action" value="Cancel" /></p>
</form>
</body>
</html>
```

Next, make the input form for a suggestion. A suggestion will be a large block of text. It will also belong to a particular section of the style guide. The section options will be limited to General, HTML, CSS, PHP, and SQL. The below code should be put in *suggestion-new.html*.

```html
<html>
<head><title>Add Suggestion</title></head>
<body>
<p>Please add a suggestion for the Style Guide
    below.</p>
<form action="suggestion-save.php"
    method="post">
<p>Section:
<select name="section">
<option>General</option>
<option>HTML</option>
<option>CSS</option>
<option>PHP</option>
<option>SQL</option>
</select></p>
```

```
<p><textarea name="suggestion" cols="80"
    rows="40"></textarea></p>
<p><input type="submit" name="submit"
    value="Save"/> <input type="submit" name=
    "submit" value="Cancel"/></p>
</body>
</html>
```

And finally, the index page. Our hypothetical management has decided that our page should have our company logo and name. They have provided us with a logo file to use: a white pen on a transparent background. Prominently displayed should be the hypothetical company name: Pendity Software. Put the following into a file named *index.html*:

```
<html>
<head><title>Pendity Software Style Guide
    </title></head>
<body>
<div><img src="logo.png"/><p>Pendity
    Software</p></div>
<div><h1>Pendity Software</h1>
<h2>Style Guide</h2></div>
<div>
<p><a href="suggestion-new.html">New
    Suggestion</a></p>
<p>Admin Only!<br/>
<a href="user-new.html">New User</a>
    </p></div>
<div>This is the page for the style guide.
</body>
</html>
```

Obviously, the index page is incomplete. We'll get back to that. For now, let's see how it looks.

First, the index (Figure 1.5):

Wow. That looks terrible. At least the links are there. Click through to each of those pages. (You will need to use the browser's Back button to

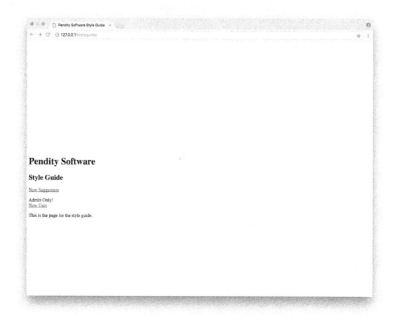

Figure 1.5. "index.html" displayed in a web browser

return to the index page. What happens if you try to submit either form?) It's time to move on to the next chapter.

FURTHER READING

This section encompasses only a very small subset of the complete HTML spec.
It contains the most basic explanation of the most common HTML elements and ideas.

The full HTML 5 specification can be found here:

https://www.w3.org/html/

The Mozilla Development Network has many tutorials and references for HTML:

https://developer.mozilla.org/en-US/docs/Web/HTML

CHAPTER 2

Cascading Style Sheets (CSS)

Originally, both content and presentation were part of HTML. However, as websites grew in size and complexity, it became clear the two needed to be separated. Consider the following overly simple web page:

```
<html>
<body>
<p><font color="green">Hello! And welcome to
    the website of <a href="index.html">
    <font color="red">Pendity Software</font>
    </a>!</font></p>
<p><font color="green">Please visit our new
    <a href="styleguide/"><font color="red">
    style guide</font></a>!</font></p>
</body>
</html>
```

Websites used to be written like this, but it proved to be quite prob-lematic for two overarching reasons. First, it creates a lot of duplication. Every time we want to change the color of the font (or text), it requires another tag. In fact, it requires another opening tag and another closing tag, lest our chosen font color go on forever. It's clear from our sample that paragraphs should be green and links should be red. While it's not too troublesome for one page and two paragraphs, imagine doing that for a website with hundreds of pages. Second, imagine the day that our boss comes in, realizes that green text with red links looks terrible, and wants it changed. How many font tags would we need to change? How many instances of "green" would we find and replace?

And so Cascading Style Sheets (CSS) was developed. CSS, which separates the style or presentation of a website from its content, offers two major advantages: It allows the same style to be applied to many elements, and it allows a given style to be easily changed. It does so by using *selectors* to match style declarations to elements, assigning the *properties* of the matched elements the corresponding *values* in the declaration block. Our page above could be rewritten as follows:

```
<html>
<head>
<style>
    p {color: green}
    a {color: red}
</style>
</head>
<body>
    <p>Hello! And welcome to the website of
    <a href="index.html">Pendity Software</a>
    !</p>
    <p>Please visit our new <a href=
    "styleguide/">style guide</a>!</p>
</body>
</html>
```

Already it looks much cleaner. However, if this style were to apply to all pages, we would split it out into a separate file.

In a file called *style.css*:

```
p {color: green}
a {color: red}
```

And then, in our HTML file above, we would replace the <head> tag with:

```
<head>
    <link rel="stylesheet" type="text/css"
    href="style.css"/>
</head>
```

Including that <link> element in every page in our website causes its style to apply to every page. And that, in a nutshell, is why CSS exists.

CSS SYNTAX

As seen in the introduction, a CSS declaration consists of two parts: The *selector* and the *declaration block*. The selector specifies what elements the declaration block should apply to, and the declaration block consists of one or more declarations, separated by semicolons. Each declaration is comprised of a property, followed by a colon, then the value for that property. For example, to revisit the link style above, consider the following declaration:

```
a {
    color: red;
    text-decoration: none;
}
```

In this example, *a* is the selector. It indicates the style should apply to all instances of the <a> tag. The braces denote the declaration block, which contains two declarations: first, that the color of the content should be red; and second, that the text should not be decorated (that is, there should be no underline). CSS declarations override the default browser behavior, so to both change the default color of a link, and to remove the underline most browsers put in by default, both the *color* and *text-decoration* properties are set.

As with HTML, a browser will try to make as much sense of a CSS declaration as possible. If it comes across a property it does not understand, it will ignore it. If it can't parse a declaration block, other CSS declaration blocks will still be parsed.

SELECTORS

A selector is not limited to applying to whole swaths of elements. The selector syntax in CSS is powerful and allows for endlessly specific declarations. The table below provides a list of the most common CSS selectors. They can be categorized into element selectors, attribute selectors, and pseudo-classes. Note that despite this distinction, it is always an HTML element that the declaration applies to.

Selector token	Function	Example	What the example selects
Class/id selectors			
. (period)	Class	.red	Any element whose class is "red"
#	id	#pageheader	The element whose id is "pageheader"
Element selectors			
*	Select all	*	Everything
element	Match *element*	p	All \<p\> elements
, (comma)	Multiple	h1,h2,h3	Any \<h1\>, \<h2\>, or \<h3\> element
Space	Descendant	div span	\<span\> elements anywhere inside any \<div\>
>	Child	p>span	\<span\> elements whose immediate parent is a \<p\>
+	Following	table + p	A \<p\> element immediately after a \<table\> element
~	Preceding	p ~ hr	A \<p\> element immediately before an \<hr\> element
Attribute selectors			
[*attribute*]	*attribute* exists	[disabled]	any disabled element
[*attribute*=*value*]	*attribute* match	[name=user]	any element where the *name* is *user*

Selector token	Function	Example	What the example selects
Pseudo-classes			
:link	unvisited links	a:link	Any <a> element the user has not visited
:hover	mouse hover	a:hover	The <a> element the user has the mouse over
:active	while clicked	a:active	An <a> element the using is clicking on
:visited	visited link	a:visited	An <a> element the user has visited
:focus	focused item	input:focus	An input element the user is using
:nth-child(*n*)	nth item	:nth-child(2)	Any element that is the second child of its parent

You are not limited to one selector; they can be combined. Consider, for example, the following CSS:

```
table.checkerboard {
    border: none;
    border-collapse: collapse;
}
    table.checkerboard tr:nth-child(odd)
    td:nth-child(odd) {
    background-color: black;
}
table.checkerboard tr:nth-child(even)
    td:nth-child(even) {
    background-color: black;
}
```

```
table.checkerboard td {
    height: 40px;
    width: 40px;
    background-color: red;
    padding: 0px;
}
```

Take a moment to create a file. Put the above CSS in the <head> of the file. In the <body>, create a table, assign it the class "checkerboard", and create eight rows containing eight cells each (Figure 2.1). View it in your browser. (The class name gives away what it looks like, doesn't it!)

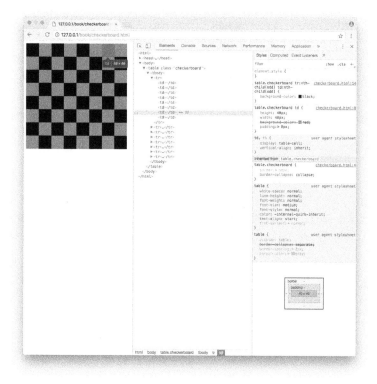

Figure 2.1. "Checkerboard.html in a web browser"

There is a wealth of information in the image above, where we have inspected the seventh cell of the first row. On the left is the actual web page showing the selected element (a <td>) and its size (a width of 40 pixels and a height of 40 pixels). The middle pane shows how the selected element appears in the document. Note that the triangles can be clicked to expand or collapse elements. The right shows all of the properties the browser considers when deciding how to display the element. The most interesting interaction is in the two declarations below "element. style". The element in question is indeed in an odd-numbered cell (7) in an odd-numbered row (1), so the background-color is black. Below it, the cell has a height and width of 40 pixels because all <td>s of checkerboard tables have those dimensions. There are also other declarations we didn't put there, labeled as coming from the "user agent stylesheet". Hmm . . .

THE CASCADE

Take a step back. In the screenshot above, some properties are crossed out and replaced with others. How does the browser know how to do this? Which ones win? The answer leads us to the core of CSS: the *cascade*, from which CSS takes its name.

The cascade is comprised of three parts: *importance*, *specificity*, and *source order*. These are evaluated in this order, and only if two conflicting declarations for the same property have the same value for a given part does the cascade use the next part to determine the style to apply.

IMPORTANCE

Importance in CSS is a mixture of two things: where the declaration comes from, and whether or not the declaration has "!important" after it. There are three types of style sheets: user agent style sheets, user style sheets, and author style sheets.

User agent style sheets are the browser's default behavior. Each browser styles elements as they see fit, but some behaviors are common. Text is usually black. Links are usually blue. Paragraphs have some space above and below them. Tables have slightly separated cells.

User style sheets are style sheets that the user creates. Google Chrome dropped support for these in early 2014, but Chrome extensions enable the same functionality. Other browsers, such as Apple Safari or Firefox, allow users to use a style sheet to override user agent defaults.

Author style sheets are the site-specific style sheets the web developer creates that are included in or with the HTML.

A declaration with !important takes precedence over any of these, but in reverse order, therefore, in order from *most* to *least* important:

1. User agent style sheet, !important
2. User style sheet, !important

3. Author style sheet, !important
4. Author style sheet
5. User style sheet
6. User agent style sheet

For example, if you absolutely wanted every <p> tag on a page to have purple text, regardless of the paragraph's id, class, or other characteristics, p {color: purple !important} would do that.

In practice, very rarely will anything override an author style sheet declaration. Users do not typically use a custom style sheet, and *!important* is not generally used. Using *!important* causes confusion, as a very specific style is ignored in favor of an "important" one.

SPECIFICITY

Given that *!important* is not generally used, and that as authors, our style sheet overrides the user's and user agent's, it is usually whichever declaration is the *most specific* that is applied. The exact rules used to determine which declaration is most specific are quite complicated, but they can be summed up with a few guidelines.

1. Any declaration in the *style* attribute of an element takes precedence over anything declared elsewhere. If your HTML file contains <p style="color: green">Some text</p>, then "Some text" will absolutely be green, regardless of however you have the <p> element styled elsewhere. (However, if that paragraph contains other elements, such as a link, they will use their own style, not inherit this one.)
2. Identifying an element using its *id* is of high precedence. If your HTML contains <p id="header" class="article">, then for any properties declared for both the *header* id and the *article* class, the property styles in the *header* id win.
3. Identifying an element using its *class* is of medium precedence. <p class="article"> will use the styling defined in the *article* class over any other <p> tag styling that lacks a class.
4. The more elements that are in the declaration, the more specific the declaration is. div table td {background-color: blue} is more specific than table td {background-color: green}; if both were in our CSS, table cells would have a background of green, unless the table was inside a <div> element, in which case they would be blue.

CODE ORDER

Code order simply states that if we declare the same thing twice, all other things being equal, the one that appears last wins. For example, if our CSS contains this:

```
p {
    color: blue;
}
p {
    color: red;
}
```

then paragraphs would be red. They have the same importance and the same specificity, but the red declaration comes last.

PROPERTIES

Some of the more obvious properties have already been used in the examples illustrating how selectors work, but CSS offers so much more. You should by now be familiar with the idea that within a declaration block there are one or more property–value pairs. Before examining more CSS properties, however, some types of values are worth mentioning. Two types of values are used to specify many properties in CSS: *color* values and *length* values.

COLORS

CSS supports the following kinds of color values:

- Keyword: Common color names such as *red*, *blue*, *black*, or *white*. There are 140 keyword colors recognized by CSS, as listed at www. w3schools.com/cssref/css_colors.asp. CSS also supports the key-word *transparent*, which means exactly what you would expect.
- RGB: Color values can be specified with rgb(*red*, *green*, *blue*). The values for red, green, and blue can be either an integer from *0* to *255* or a percentage from *0%* to *100%*, but they cannot be used in the same rgb() value. As an example, both rgb(255, 0, 0) and rgb(100%, 0%, 0%) produce a solid red.

- RGBA: Color values can also be specified with an alpha channel to allow colors to blend. The alpha value is the fourth parameter and must always be a number between *0.0* and *1.0*, where *0* is fully transparent and *1* is fully opaque. As with rgb(), the first three values must all be either integers between *0* and *255* or a percentage. A declaration such as background-color: rgba(255, 0, 0, 0.25); on an element with a white background behind it would produce a pink background.

- Hex: Colors can also be specified as hex values such as *#ff0000*. The first two hexadecimal digits correspond to the red component, the second two to green, and the last two to blue. Thus, *#ff0000* is red, and *#0000ff* is blue. Additionally, values may be specified using only three hexadecimal digits. Black could be specified as *#000*, which the browser interprets as *#000000*. Likewise, *#f00* is also red, *#00f* is also blue, and *#fff* is white. The letters are not case-sensitive; *#F00* is red as well.

- HSL: Instead of RGB, which is useful to computers, colors can also be specified using HSL syntax, which may be more intuitive to people. HSL stands for *hue*, *saturation*, and *lightness*. The syntax is similar to RGB syntax: hsl(0, 100%, 50%). However, the values are completely different. The first value is the hue. The hue is the number of degrees counterclockwise around the color wheel and is specified as a number. (Any number are allowed, but as it is a circle, any number outside the range of 0 to 360 is the same as some number in that range.) A value of *0* corresponds to red, *120* is green, and *240* is blue, and *360* returns us to red. The second value is the saturation, expressed as a percentage between *0%* and *100%*, and specifies how intense the color is. A value of *0%* is gray (no color saturation), and a value of *100%* is fully the color specified by the hue. The last value is the lightness, also expressed as a percentage, and specifies how close to black or white the color is. A value of *0%* is fully black, *100%* is fully white, and *50%* is the exactly the color specified by the hue and saturation values. Our value above, *hsl(0, 100%, 50%)*, is once again our example color red. Red hue, full saturation, and precisely in the middle of lightness, leaning neither toward black or white. You may find HSL easier to use, as once you have the color you're looking for, it's much easier to find the exact shade by changing the saturation and lightness. If you start with blue, *hsl(240, 100%, 50%)*, you might decide to gray it out: *hsl(240, 35%, 50)*, then make it lighter: *hsl(240, 35%, 75%)* to end up with a pale blue-gray color. The corresponding hex rgb code is *rgb(169, 169, 214)*, which is much more tedious to figure out. A good HSL color picker is available at, appropriately, http://hslpicker.com.

- HSLA: As with RGBA, HSL is also available with an alpha channel. The first three values are the HSL values, and the last value is the alpha channel.

LENGTH UNITS

Length values are the other common CSS property value. As with colors, they can be expressed in a variety of ways. All length values take a number and a unit, with no space in between. When the number is 0, the unit may be omitted.

- **px**: Pixels. A pixel is equal to 1/96th of an inch. Modern computer displays typically have a higher resolution but one px is 1/96th of an inch measurement in CSS.
- **in**, **cm**, **mm**: Short for inch, centimeter, and millimeters, respectively. These are not generally used for screen output, though they can be useful when working with printing.
- **pt**: Points, which are 1/72 of an inch. Although can be used to specify any length, this is most likely to be used to specify the size of text; for example, font-size: 24pt would result in a 24-point font.
- **em**: This unit is relative to the size of the font used within the element. *1em* is approximately the width of the letter M in the current font.
- **vw**: Viewport width. The viewport is the browser window (or when printing, the page). The number used specified the percentage of the current width of the viewport, so *50vw* is a value equal to half the width of the browser window (not including non-browsing areas, such as scroll bars). This value changes and is recomputed when the user changes the width of the browser window.
- **vh**: Viewport height. This works the same way as vw but uses the current height of the browser window instead (again, not including things such as the title bar, scroll bar, etc.).
- **%**: A length may be specified as a percentage of the content space of its parent element.

PROPERTY LIST

Properties, as we've seen, define specific behaviors for the visual presentation of our content. Below is a list of the most common properties used, arranged by type. When a property uses a color value, as defined above, it is shortened as *<color>* below. Likewise, length values are shortened as *<length>*. Most properties also take the special values *initial*, which sets the property to its default value, and *inherit*, which explicitly says to use the value of the parent element. For brevity, these values are not listed individually below.

Color Properties

color: Sets the color of the text in the element.
Allowed Values: *<color>*
Default: Not specified. Generally, user agents style text as black, links as blue, and visited links as purple.
background-color: Sets the background color of the element, which will paint the background of the element (including the padding spacing, see below) with the *<color>* specified.
Allowed Values: *<color>*, including *transparent*
Default: *transparent*, allowing the background of parent elements to show through.

Font (Text) Properties

font-family: The font or family of fonts text should be displayed in.
Allowed Values: Either a specific font family name, such as *Times* or *Courier*, or a generic family name, such as *serif, sans-serif*, or *monospace*. If a font name has spaces, it must be quoted, such as *"Times New Roman"*.
Default: Varies, depending on the user agent.
The *font-family* property allows for multiple fonts to be declared at the same time. The user agent will use the first one it understands. Because of this behavior, if using a specific font, it is best to follow the declaration with a generic family name. If the specific font is not available, the browser will use a font available to it in the generic family. For example:

```
p {
    font-family: "Times New Roman", Times,
    serif;
}
```

In the declaration above, the browser will use the *Times New Roman* font if it is available to it. If not, it will attempt to use the *Times* font. If neither font is available, it will use any serif font it can find.

font-size: The size of the font to use.

Allowed Values: *<length>*, though usually expressed in points, pixels, or % of parent's size. Fonts can also be set to any of the following keywords, though they are not often used: *xx-small*, *x-small, small, medium, large, x-large, xx-large.*

Default: *medium*. Generally, this is about 12 points.

font-weight: The thickness of the text.

Allowed Values: Any of the following: *normal, bold, bolder, lighter*, or a multiple of 100 between 100 and 900. A value of *400* is equal to *normal*, and *700* is equal to *bold*.

Default: *normal* (400)

This is usually either *normal* or *bold*, so it may be thought of as toggling the font's boldness on.

font-style: Whether the font is italicized.

Allowed Values: Any of the following: *normal, italic, oblique*

Default: *normal*

In theory, *oblique* and *italic* may be different. A font can have a specific typeface for each value. In practice, they are generally the same, and *oblique* is almost never used.

text-decoration: Whether to add a line to the text.

Allowed Values: *none, underline, overline, line-through*

Default: *none*

Generally used to underline text (such as in links), the *text-decoration* property can also be used to draw a line through the text so it appears crossed out using *line-through*. The *overline* value is not common.

text-align: How to horizontally align the text.

Allowed values: *left, right, center, justify*

Default: Left (unless the language reads right to left)

Recall that a block element spans the full width allotted to it. To center text within such a block element, *text-align* would be set to *center*. User agents typically do this for header tags (*<h1>*, *<h2>*, etc.). A value of *justify* stretches the text to line up on both sides, as in books or in newspapers.

vertical-align: How to vertically align the text.

Allowed Values: *baseline, <length>, sub, super, top, middle, bottom*

Default: *baseline*, but user agents usually change table cells to *middle*.

The *vertical-align* is most often used to align text within tall table cells. Most browsers align text in table cells to the middle of the cell, but this can be changed with either *top* or *bottom*. Elements that occur inside text align to the text's *baseline*, but a span of text can be set to act as subscript or superscript with *sub* or *super*, respectively. An element (such as a span) can use a *<length>* value with the *vertical-align* property to move the text up by the length specified. (Negative values move the element down.) While this can be used to align an image with text, the image only takes up one line of text; another property (*float*, below) is usually used instead.

white-space: How to treat whitespace such as space, tabs, and newlines (returns).

Allowed Values: *normal, nowrap, pre, pre-wrap, pre-line*

Default: *normal*

When *normal*, all consecutive whitespace is treated as a single space. If your content contains a newline, a tab character, and seven spaces next to each other, it renders as a space. (Recall that a *
* element is typically used to create a new line in content.) A value of *nowrap* acts much like normal, except text will never wrap unless a <br> is found. Using *pre* makes the element act like a *<pre>* tag in HTML, except the font does not change; spaces are left intact and lines do not wrap unless a newline character is encountered. Setting this to *pre-wrap* preserves whitespace but allows the text to wrap to fit the element's box. Finally, *pre-line* acts like *normal*, but text will wrap on newline characters.

Size Properties

height: The height of an element.

Allowed Values: *auto*, *<length>* (non-negative)

Default: *auto*

When the height of an element is *auto*, the browser calculates the minimum height needed to display an element and its contents and uses that as the element's height.

width: The width of an element.

Allowed Values: *auto*, *<length>* (non-negative)

Default: *auto*

For inline elements, *auto* is the minimum width needed to display an element's contents. For block elements, *auto* is usually equal to 100 percent of the width of its parent. Note that tables, while described in the HTML chapter as a block element, actually have their own display definition and will use only as much width as necessary to display the contents inside.

max-height, max-width: The maximum height and width of an element.

Allowed Values: *none, <length>* (non-negative)

Default: *none*

With *max-height* and *max-width*, elements can be restricted in the amount of space they can consume. If an element does not need the full space, it does not use it, but it is not allowed to exceed the dimension specified.

min-height, min-width: The minimum height and width of an object.

Allowed Values: *<length>* (non-negative)

Default: *0*

Elements can also be given minimum dimensions that they must adhere to.

Box Model Properties

The box model is explained in detail later in this chapter.

margin: The margin to leave around the border of the element.

Allowed Values: One to four *<length>*s.

Default: *0*, although many browsers specify defaults for different elements.

The *margin* property takes one to four values. If provided one value, all four margins are set equal to it. If given two values, the top and bottom margins are set to the first value, and the left and right margins are set to the second. For three values, the bottom margin becomes the third value. With four values, the fourth value specifies the right margin. An easy way to remember this rule is to start at the top of a box and work clockwise, bouncing back and forth across the value list. If an element has the declaration margin: 2em 1em 3em; the top margin is 2em, the right is 1em, the bottom is 3em, and for the left margin, we bounce back to the 1em value.

The property *margin* is actually shorthand for setting each margin property individually. Margins can also be set using *margin-top, margin-right, margin-bottom,* and *margin-left*. Individual properties may be handy when only changing or overriding one side.

border-width: The width of the border around an element.

Allowed Values: One to four values of *<length>, thin, medium, thick*

Default: *medium*

The *border-width* property is one of three properties that define the look of a border. As with *margin*, above, it accepts one to four values, corresponding to the same sides as in the *margin* property.

The border width can also be set for each side independently using *border-top-width*, *border-right-width*, *border-bottom-width*, and *border-left-width*.

border-style: The style of the border around an element.

Allowed Values: *none, hidden, dotted, dashed, solid, double, groove, ridge, inset, outset*

Default: *none*, although some browsers override this for <*table*> elements.

Although many values are allowed for the border style, only three are typically used in practice: *none*, *solid*, and *hidden*. The others are visually distracting. A value of *solid* is simply a solid line; *none* means no border; *hidden*, like *none*, means no border, but unlike *none*, if a border is *hidden*, it means it's more important than another border declaration. Consider the following snippet:

```
<table style="border-collapse: collapse">
<tr style="border-style: solid">
<td style="border-style: none">TD 1</td>
<td style="border-style: hidden">TD 2</td>
<td style="border-style: solid">TD 3</td>
</tr>
</table>
```

If we came across this table, the table would be drawn with the browser default border. The row would be drawn with a solid border, which would trump the table border, as we specified it. The first cell would have no border on the right side, as the solid style of the table row "wins" on the top, bottom, and left. The second cell would have no border on *any* side because *hidden* takes precedence over other border styles. The third cell would have no border on the left side but would on the top, bottom, and right.

As width *border-width*, *border-style* may be specified individually using *border-top-style*, *border-right-style*, *border-bottom-style*, and *border-left-style*.

border-color: The color of an element's border.

Allowed Values: One to four <*color*> values, including *transparent*

Default: The color of the element's text, as defined with *color*.

As with the width and style, the color may have one to four values corresponding to the same sides, and as with the width and style, may be specified individually using *border-top-color*, *border-right-color*, *border-bottom-color*, and *border-left-color*.

border: Shorthand property to define a full border.

Allowed Values: Requires the properties for a border width, style, and color, as defined above.

Default: The defaults are the same values as the individual properties above.

Unlike the individual properties, the *border* property only accepts one set of values. Therefore, a style set with *border* applies to all four borders. However, this shorthand property can be defined for individual sides using *border-top*, *border-right*, *border-bottom*, and *border-left*.

border-collapse: Whether table cells should have space between them.

Allowed Values: *separate, collapse*

Default: *separate*

With the default value of *separate*, browsers will leave space between table cells, and borders for table rows will not be drawn. With the value of *collapse*, no space is left between table cells, or between table cells and the edge of the table itself, and borders (and other properties such as *background-color*!) for table rows are honored.

padding: The space between border of an element and the content inside it.

Allowed Values: One to four *<length>* values (non-negative)

Default: *0*, although user agent style sheets have defaults for many elements.

As with *margin*, *padding* allows for one to four values and follows the same method when applying them to each side. Sides may be specified individually with *padding-top*, *padding-right*, *padding-bottom*, and *padding-left*.

box-sizing: How to measure the height and width of an element

Allowed Values: *content-box, border-box*

Default: *content-box*

By default, when specifying that an element should have a width of 500px, this defines the amount of space that the element's content will be given. The space used by the element's padding and border are in addition to that value. If this property is set to *border-box*, any width or height specified instead refer to the total of the content, padding, and border. The content width is then calculated by subtracting the border and padding from the given width.

Display and Visibility Properties

display: Whether (and how) to render an element.

Allowed Values: *block, inline, inline-block, table, table-row, table-cell, none*

Default: *inline*, although user agent style sheets have defaults for many elements.

The *display* property allows elements to be rendered like a different element.

Both *block* and *inline* should be familiar by now.

inline-block acts like an inline element but permits setting height and width, which are otherwise only able to be set for block elements.

The *none* value hides an element completely; it does not show to the user and takes no space in the page layout.

The *table, table-row*, and *table-cell* values act like *<table>*, *<tr>*, and *<td>* elements, respectively, and are the preferred method for creating a table layout that is not semantically tabular data. As with true tables, an element with display: table-cell should be the child of an element with display: table-row, which in turn should be the child of an element with display: table.

visibility: Whether an element is visible.

Allowed Values: *visible, hidden*

Default: *visible*

Whereas the visibility of an element would seem self-explanatory, this raises the question: why does visibility: hidden exist if display: none exists as well? The answer is that unlike setting an element's *display* property to *none*, when setting the *visibility* property to *hidden*, the element still takes up space in the page layout. That is, it's still there; the user just can't see it.

overflow: What to do if an element's content exceeds its dimensions.

Allowed Values: *visible, hidden, scroll, auto*

Default: *visible*

If an element has a specified height and width, and its content exceeds those dimensions, this property determines what happens to the content.

If this property is *visible*, the content overflows the element's box, essentially ignoring the element's dimensions.

If *hidden*, the overflowing content is simply invisible.

If set to *scroll*, scrollbars are added to the element to allow the user to scroll.

If set to *auto*, scrollbars are only added if scrolling is necessary to see the entire content.

text-overflow: How to signal the content overflowed the element.
Allowed Values: *clip, ellipsis, <provided string>*
Default: *clip*
The default, *clip*, means that no indication is given to the user when text overflows an element.
A value of *ellipsis* will shorten the text as necessary to allow an ellipsis to be added.
Alternatively, the page author may provide a custom string to use.

Positioning Properties

position: Where on the page to put the element
Allowed Values: *static, relative, absolute, fixed*
Default: *static*
The default, *static*, simply means to position the element as normal, according to its position in the document, and is the method all examples to this point have used.
Its cousin, *relative*, acts much like *static*, except after positioning the element according to normal flow, the position of the element is adjusted.
A value of *absolute* changes the element to be positioned relative to its first ancestor not set to *static* or to the entire document if no such ancestor exists. (An element may be set to *relative* simply to not be a static element.)
Finally, *fixed* positions an element relative to the browser window. Unlike any other value, *fixed* elements do not scroll with the rest of the page.
This property is used in tandem with the following properties.
top, left, bottom, right: Used with *position* to move and place elements.
Allowed Values: *auto, <length>*
Default: *auto*
Each of these properties specifies a length from an edge at which to place the element's edge. The behavior is slightly different depending on the value of *position*. Keep in mind that for each of these, the default value of *auto* means to let the browser figure out on its own what the best value is, which will usually depend on the content inside the element.
If the position is *static*, these properties are ignored.
For a position of *relative*, these properties "push" the element inward from the direction of the property. For example, an element with position: relative; left: 20px would be laid out as normal, but the

element would be "pushed" from the left (i.e., to the right) by 20 pixels.

If the position is *absolute*, these properties specify how far away from the edge of its non-static ancestor the edge of this element should be.

If the position is *fixed*, these properties specify how far away from the edges of the browser window this element should be.

Examples of *absolute* and *fixed* can be found in the project at the end of this chapter.

THE BOX MODEL

As far as CSS is concerned, every element is a box. The browser window (or paper, when printing) is a box (Figure 2.2). Block elements are boxes that take up the entire width of their containing element, and inline elements are boxes that exist within the flow of the document. Place the following in a file to examine how the box model works:

```
<html>
<head>
<style>
div {
    width: 600px;
    border: lightgray solid 1px;
}
p {
    width: 400px;
    height: 200px;
    border: green solid 3px;
    margin-left: 3em;
    padding: 1.5em;
    background-color: yellow;
}
span {
    position: relative;
    top: 1em;
    border: blue solid 1px;
}
#absolute {
```

```
    width: 200px;
    position: absolute;
    top: 200px;
    left: 200px;
    border: red solid 1px;
}
</style>
</head>
<body>
<div>
<p>Here we have some <span>sample text
    </span>.</p>
</div>
<div id="absolute">
A bit of text in this one, too.
</div>
</body>
</html>
```

Open it in a browser and inspect the <p> tag.

Figure 2.2. Desc: "The box model in a web browser"

The diagram on the right side, underneath the style declarations, is how the browser interpreted the element according to the CSS box model. Note that all sizes are in pixels, and the diagram is clearly not to scale. For the <p> element, we specified 400 pixels by 200 pixels, which defines the size of the content area. A padding of 1.5em translates to 24 pixels. The border is 3 pixels wide, the top and bottom margins are 1em, or 16 pixels, as defined by the user agent, and the left margin is 3em, or 48 pixels, as specified in the document. The right margin was calculated automatically from the amount of space inside the <div>. Note that when mousing over the <p> tag and the containing <div>, the orange area of the <p> tag (the area including the margins) matches the blue area of the <div> (the area specifying the content).

Likewise, the <div> was given a set width, and by default is left justified, so its extra margin is on its right side as well. Mouse over the <body> tag in the middle panel to see why the border of the <div> doesn't reach any edge of the page: Chrome defines the body tag with an 8-pixel margin on all sides.

Inspect the <span> element, which has a blue border, and another box appears. The positioning box informs us that because the element has *position: relative*, the top of the element was pushed 16 pixels (1em) down from the top (and the bottom of the element was pushed −16 pixels up from the bottom, i.e., 16 pixels down as well).

The absolutely positioned <div>, with the red border, also has a positioning box in its diagram. Its position is relative to its closest non-static ancestor, the <html> element. (The <body> tag, although it is its parent, is using static positioning, so the 8-pixel margins are ignored.) In the screen shot, the web page is displayed in an area 635 pixels wide by 955 pixels tall. Chrome rendered the text inside at 18 pixels high, and a content width of 200 pixels was specified, and there is a 1-pixel border on all sides. The element was placed 200 pixels away from the top and left of the <html> element, and the right and bottom positioning was calculated from these values. $635 - 200 - 1 - 200 - 1$ results in 233 pixels on the right side; $955 - 200 - 1 - 18 - 1$ leaves 735 pixels on the bottom. When looking at this example in a window of a different size, some of the numbers will be different, but the calculations for the box model will remain the same.

So, to reiterate, unless it is static (automatically positioned), first the element is positioned. Then, the margin is the space added outside the border. The padding is the space added inside the border, and the content is the area available to text or other elements inside the padding.

COMMENTS

CSS also allows for the use of comments. In CSS, comments start with /* and end with */ and may span multiple lines. Note that while this is the same block comment style found in other languages, there is no single line comment in CSS. You must use /* and */ for all comments, even those on a single line.

```
.warning {
    color: red;
    background-color: yellow;/* Red on yellow
    is terrible! */
}
```

WORKING WITH DIFFICULT BROWSERS

CSS seems like a fantastic method for laying out your page. And by and large, it is. There's just one problem. Browsers vary in their support for the standard. Internet Explorer (IE), for example, does not understand the *initial* keyword at all.

In such a case, the easiest answer is to declare the same property multiple times. For example, if most of the links on a website are internal links and colored red, we might have a declaration as such:

```
a {
    color: red;
}
```

However, in a few specific places, there are links to an external site that should use the browser's default color. In most browsers, color: initial would work, but IE wouldn't understand that. However, because browsers ignore declarations they don't understand, both can be specified:

```
a {
    color: red;
}
```

```
a.external {
    color: blue;
    color: initial;
}
```

With this styling, most links will be red. If a link is given the class *external*, it is set to blue. Then, it is set to *initial* in any browser that understands that value. Links are usually blue anyway, but if a visitor has a user style sheet, or if the browser's default isn't quite "blue", those values are used instead.

Now let's revisit the previous pages of the project to make them more attractive.

PROJECT

Our index page is ugly and completely nonfunctional. Some CSS will fix that. First, the index page must be updated to add some *id*s to the div elements. Change the index page to look like it does below. We're adding some *id* attributes to the div elements and linking to an as yet non-existent style sheet in the header.

```
<html>
<head>
<title>Pendity Software Style Guide
    </title>
<link rel="stylesheet" type="text/css"
    href="style.css"/>
</head>
<body>
<div id="icon"><img src="logo.png"/>
    </div>
<div id="header">
<h1>Pendity Software</h1>
<h2>Style Guide</h2>
</div>
<div id="links">
<a href="suggestion-new.html">New
    Suggestion</a>
```

```
<p>Admin Only!</p>
<a href="user-new.html">New User</a>
</div>
<div id="main">
<p>This is the page for the style guide.
    </p>
</div>
</body>
</html>
```

What we next want to do is lay out each section and apply some color and text styling. The below CSS will accomplish this. Save the below in a file called *style.css* and place it in the same directory as the index file.

```
* {
    box-sizing: border-box;
}
body, div {
    margin: 0;
    padding: 0;
}
body {
    background-color: #500;
}
#icon {
    position: absolute;
    height: 8em;
    width: 8em;
}
#icon img {
    margin: 0.5em;
    height: 7em;
    width: 7em;
}
#header {
    position: absolute;
    left: 8em;
    top: 0;
    width: calc(100% - 8em);
```

```
        height: 8em;
        color: white;
        text-align: center;
        font-family: cursive;
    }
    #header h1 {
        margin-bottom: 0;
    }
    #header h2 {
        position: relative;
        left: 5em;
        margin-top: 0;
        display: inline-block;
    }
    #links {
        position: absolute;
        top: 8em;
        left: 0;
        width: 8em;
        padding-top: 1em;
        height: calc(100% - 8em);
        padding: 0.5em;
        color: #aaa;
    }
    #links a {
        color: white;
        text-decoration: none;
    }
    #links a:hover {
        text-decoration: underline;
    }
    #main {
        background-color: white;
        position: absolute;
        top: 8em;
        left: 8em;
        min-height: calc(100% - 8em);
        width: calc(100% - 8em);
        padding: 0.5em;
    }
```

Take some time to inspect the resulting page. See if you can answer the following questions:

1. Why does *#main* have a width of *calc(100% − 8em)*?
2. Why does #main have a *min-height* declaration, instead of a *height* declaration? (Hint: What happens if you add many lines of text that go beyond the height of the browser window and use *height* instead?)
3. Why does *#icon img* have an explicit height and width declared?
4. In *#header h2*, what behavior does *display: inline-block* prevent?

Overall, this is a pretty good style sheet. There's just one little hiccup that seems a little wrong. When you resize the browser window, you see bits of red near the edge of the window. The reason is that there's a bit of a delay between the operating system redrawing the window and the CSS recalculating the size of *div#main*. It's not much, but it's enough that the red background shows up before the div paints it white. Is there another way to get this look?

Several, actually. The first and easiest answer is that we don't really want a specific height on each div. Rather, we want it to go to the edge. Remove the height and width properties for any element that has the calc() function in them, and replace them with *right* and *bottom* declarations. Also, move the *background-color* declaration from the body to each individual element that should be this color, that is, *#icon*, *#header*, and *#links*.

The net result should be this:

```
*  {
    box-sizing: border-box;
}
body, div {
    margin: 0;
    padding: 0;
}
#icon {
    position: absolute;
    height: 8em;
    width: 8em;
    background-color: #500;
}
#icon img {
    margin: 0.5em;
    height: 7em;
```

```css
        width: 7em;
}
#header {
    position: absolute;
    left: 8em;
    top: 0;
    right: 0;
    height: 8em;
    color: white;
    text-align: center;
    font-family: cursive;
    background-color: #500;
}
#header h1 {
    margin-bottom: 0;
}
#header h2 {
    position: relative;
    left: 5em;
    margin-top: 0;
    display: inline-block;
}
#links {
    position: absolute;
    top: 8em;
    left: 0;
    width: 8em;
    padding-top: 1em;
    bottom: 0;
    padding: 0.5em;
    color: #aaa;
    background-color: #500;
}
#links a {
    color: white;
    text-decoration: none;
}
#links a:hover {
    text-decoration: underline;
}
```

```
#main {
    position: absolute;
    top: 8em;
    left: 8em;
    right: 0;
    bottom: 0;
    padding: 0.5em;
}
```

This accomplishes the same result as our original style. It does mean that changing the size of the window draws white where we would really like red, but that's less noticeable than the other way around. It does, however, eliminate the need for calc and hopefully makes the layout clearer to us as we read it.

Finally, one more example to illustrate how the same look can be achieved multiple ways. Take a look at the style below:

```
* {
    box-sizing: border-box;
}
body, div {
    margin: 0;
    padding: 0;
}
#icon {
    position: absolute;
    height: 8em;
    width: 8em;
    background-color: #500;
    z-index: 4;
}
#icon img {
    margin: 0.5em;
    height: 7em;
    width: 7em;
}
#header {
    position: absolute;
```

```
    left: 0;
    top: 0;
    right: 0;
    height: 8em;
    color: white;
    text-align: center;
    font-family: cursive;
    background-color: #500;
    z-index: 3;
}
#header h1 {
    margin-bottom: 0;
}
#header h2 {
    position: relative;
    left: 5em;
    margin-top: 0;
    display: inline-block;
}
#links {
    position: absolute;
    top: 0;
    left: 0;
    width: 8em;
    bottom: 0;
    padding: 0.5em;
    padding-top: 9em;
    color: #aaa;
    background-color: #500;
    z-index: 2;
}
#links a {
    color: white;
    text-decoration: none;
}
#links a:hover {
    text-decoration: underline;
}
#main {
    position: absolute;
    top: 0;
```

```
        left: 0;
        padding: 0.5em;
        padding-left: 8.5em;
        padding-top: 8.5em;
}
```

Note that in this version, all the elements start in the top left corner. They overlap. They use the *padding* directive to place the content, whereas the previous versions split them into their own *div*s. (Inspect the elements in a browser and see how they interact, or rather, don't interact.) The most noticeable difference with this version is that "Pendity Software" now appears in the center of the entire page rather than the center of the area above the main content. We could, of course, achieve *that* with another layout. We could separate the top banner into its own *div* with elements inside it and put the rest of the page, both *#links* and *#main*, in its own container *div*. That would require slightly changing the HTML.

But enough of achieving the same thing in many different ways. CSS is supposed to be about reuse and achieving multiple looks without changing the document, right? That makes it easier to update the look of the document.

The style above was popular in the early days of the web. A banner along the top, and a list of links on the left side. Today, those links are more often given a menu-like appearance just underneath the banner. We can achieve that look—again, without changing anything in the HTML file itself—with the below styles. Note that the below should replace everything including and below the *#links* block in the style sheet above.

```
#links {
    position: absolute;
    top: 8em;
    left: 0;
    right: 0;
    height: 2em;
    color: #aaa;
    background-color: #500;
    z-index: 2;
    border-top: #999 solid 1px;
    border-bottom: #999 solid 1px;
    text-align: center;
}
```

```
#links * {
    display: inline-block;
    margin-top: 0;
    padding-top: 0.25em;
}
#links a {
    margin-left: 2em;
    color: white;
    text-decoration: none;
    height: 100%;
}
#links p {
    margin-left: 5em;
}
#links a:hover {
    background-color: white;
    color: #060;
}
#main {
    margin-left: auto;
    margin-right: auto;
    max-width: 900px;
    padding-top: 10.5em;
}
```

And just like that, we have a centered list of links along a bar, with the Admin label separating the Admin link from the rest. We could add more links here simply by putting them inside the links div, and they would expand to take the space needed. We've added a maximum width to the body and centered it to make it easier to read. Perhaps we'll need more space later, but for now, this is a good baseline.

We will eventually want to apply this header and navigation to all our pages. That will be easier to do in the last chapter using PHP. For now, we need somewhere to store the information that users enter.

FURTHER READING

The latest all-in-one version of the CSS specification is available here:
https://www.w3.org/TR/CSS2/
Starting with CSS3, the specifications have been split out into multiple
specifications:
https://www.w3.org/Style/CSS/specs.en.html
Mozilla again has a very detailed and somewhat technical explanation of CSS:
https://developer.mozilla.org/en-US/docs/Web/CSS/Reference
W3Schools offers a more beginner-friendly and easier to navigate version:
Reference: https://www.w3schools.com/cssref/default.asp
Tutorial: https://www.w3schools.com/css/default.asp
For checking browser support, visit:
https://caniuse.com
An important aspect of modern web design not covered here is *responsive web
design*, used to make your page attractive and accessible from a variety of
devices:
https://www.w3schools.com/css/css_rwd_viewport.asp
CSS flexbox can be an easy way to solve page layout problems but lacks support
in older versions of IE:
https://www.w3schools.com/css/css3_flexbox.asp
https://developer.mozilla.org/en-US/docs/Web/CSS/CSS_Flexible_Box_Layout/
Basic_Concepts_of_Flexbox
Perhaps even better than flexbox, CSS grid layout provides another method for
page layout, but again, support is lacking in IE:
https://css-tricks.com/snippets/css/complete-guide-grid/
https://developer.mozilla.org/en-US/docs/Web/CSS/CSS_Grid_Layout
https://www.w3schools.com/css/css_grid.asp

CHAPTER 3

MySQL

MySQL is a database. It provides a place to store data. When a user visits a web page, whether they enter data in a form or simply look around the site, from the server's point of view, the user asks for a page, and they receive the page, and then its job is done. There is no persistence inherent in HTML.

In the early days of the web, before websites were heavily data-driven, you might see something like a visitor counter on even the most amateur of pages. Behind the scenes, these hit counters were often simply a text file that the web page would read, display, and increment. While that works fine for a single piece of data, such as how many times the page has been accessed, running a simple e-commerce website using text files would be a nightmare, and a data-intensive site such as eBay or Amazon would be outright impossible.

A relational database provides two major benefits: first, it allows for the data to be logically organized; and second, it provides a way to access only the data needed, rather than all of the data in its entirety. If Amazon needed to load all the information about every item in its inventory whenever you visited it, it would simply collapse upon itself.

WHY MYSQL?

MySQL is often used in all but the most commercial of websites for a simple reason: It's free. Although it offers many other benefits, such as built-in or third-party support in many typical web languages, an extensive feature set that has greatly improved since its early days as well as a couple MySQL-specific extensions or functions that make life for a developer much easier (GROUP_CONCAT comes to mind), MySQL is often the first database many developers start with simply because the barrier to entry is so low.

This isn't to say that MySQL isn't suited for enterprise-grade commercial development. MySQL also offers a paid version with paid support for commercial clients, but that's outside the scope of this book and a beginning developer. However, even small-scale commercial apps might find the free version of MySQL sufficient for their needs.

PHPMYADMIN

Because the free version of MySQL is decidedly light on its visual administration, a community tool called phpMyAdmin is the de facto MySQL administration tool. It can be downloaded from www.phpmyadmin.net using the top link in the upper right of the page.

Installation is straightforward: Add it to a web-accessible directory, remove the ".sample" part of the *config.sample.inc.php* file, open the file, and add a 32-character random string where it asks for a value for $cfg['blowfish_secret']. Put any 32 characters (except a single quote) in between the two single quotes. The rest of the configuration should work as is. Be sure to delete the setup folder.

Alternatively, once the phpMyAdmin folder has been added somewhere you can access it, you can go to the setup folder within the phpMyAdmin folder from within a web browser to complete setup in the browser.

Once set up, go to the main phpMyAdmin folder in a web browser. You can log in with any MySQL username and password. Once logged in, you will likely see a message at the bottom that some extended features have been disabled. Click the "Find out why" link and allow phpMyAdmin to create a database for itself.

MySQL also offers a command-line tool that may be used instead. For ease of use, we'll stick with phpMyAdmin.

THE STRUCTURE OF MYSQL

MySQL, as with other database software, is structured into four layers. At the top level is the server. The server is the machine on which our MySQL installation runs. (*Clusters*, collections of servers, are outside the scope of this book.) Each server may contain multiple *databases*. Each database may contain multiple *tables*, which in turn contain multiple rows (sets) of *fields*. A field is a single piece of data, such as a number, string, or date.

Or to describe that in reverse: In MySQL, a *field* is a single piece of data. A collection of *fields* (columns) creates a single *row*. Multiple rows (instances of a collection of fields) together create a *table*. Multiple tables together create a *database*. Multiple databases are housed on a server.

Note that the word *database* can be used to describe several things: It may refer to the *database software* itself; in our case, MySQL. It may refer to an actual database as MySQL (or other software) thinks of it: a collection of related tables. Colloquially, it may refer to what is actually a collection of databases; when referring to the "MySQL database," we might mean multiple actual databases running in MySQL.

A given server may run multiple applications on it, each of them needing to use MySQL. In our example project, we're building a style guide. The same server might host a ticketing system, a list of clients, or any number of other projects. Each project is a logical division of scope designed to fulfill a specific purpose. The correlation in MySQL is a database. There is nothing *explicitly* stopping us from creating a single database for all our projects and using a very long list of tables; it is, however, bad practice. For example, if our database software installation is used by an issue-tracking system, a style guide, and a client-accessible support forum, we would need a list of users for each of those. It makes much more sense to have three separate databases, each with their own *users* table, than to have a single database with *forum_users*, *styleguide_users*, and *issue_users*, or even worse, to try to shoehorn them all into the *same* table!

To reiterate: *A database is a collection of tables that should correspond to a single application.*

A table, meanwhile, will often refer to a specific *thing* within an application. A *users* table, for example, will contain all (or most) of the information about a user. In forum software, a *boards* table would contain all the information specific to the board as a whole. A *posts* table would contain all the information about a specific post, including which board it belongs to and which user made the post. Each table is logically structured like a table in HTML. A *field*, or column, is a piece of particular data of a certain type, and each *row* is an instance of that data. For example, a *users* table might contain a user ID, a login, a password, and the user's first and last name. For each user in our application, there would exist one row in the table containing all of their information.

For example, a *users* table might look like this (Figure 3.1):

And it might have the following structure (Figure 3.2):

Before we go any further, we should note that there are some serious issues with that users table. First among them is that passwords are stored in plain text. Passwords should *never* be stored in plain text, regardless of the size and scope of the project, if only because people have a tendency to reuse the same password in multiple places. We will address this and the other issues later. For now, however, we're simply using this as an example of a table in general.

id	username	password	firstname	lastname
1	superCool47	extraCool48	Mike	Smith
2	SmartGuy29	xmRoc397omesA3	John	Doe

Figure 3.1. Desc: A *users* table

#	Name	Type	Collation	Attributes	Null	Default	Comments	Extra
1	id	mediumint(8)		UNSIGNED	No	None		AUTO_INCREMENT
2	username	varchar(64)	latin1_swedish_ci		No	None		
3	password	varchar(64)	latin1_swedish_ci		No	None		
4	firstname	varchar(64)	latin1_swedish_ci		No	None		
5	lastname	varchar(64)	latin1_swedish_ci		No	None		

Figure 3.2. Desc: Structure of the *users* table

The above table contains two rows, one for each of our users. It contains five fields: id, login, password, firstname, and lastname. MySQL offers many different field types, and it's time to look at them in depth.

DATA (FIELD) TYPES

Data types in MySQL denote the type of data stored in a field and can be grouped into one of three categories: numeric, string, and date/time. (There are also spatial and JSON data types, which are not discussed here.)

NUMERIC DATA TYPES

Numeric data types, as the name implies, are used to store a number of some sort. Numeric data may either be an integer, a fixed-point value, a floating point value, or a bit value. Different field types offer different ranges of values but require different number of bytes to store. It is best to use the smallest possible range that will store the values needed.

Numeric data types may have an optional property, *UNSIGNED*. This property may be used to force numeric data types to be positive. When used on an integer, it also extends the range of the integer. For example, a TINYINT field normally holds a value between −128 and 127. Changing the field to TINYINT UNSIGNED changes the range to between 0 and 255. This can be useful when dealing with numbers guaranteed to be positive (such as row IDs) if the extra positive numbers prevent the use of a larger data type. However, UNSIGNED comes with a downside: If MySQL performs subtraction with at least one UNSIGNED operand, it will throw an error if the result would be negative.

MySQL supports the following integer types. Note that the minimum unsigned value for each is zero. When dealing with numbers with no fractional component, one of the integer types should be used.

Type	Bytes	Minimum signed	Maximum signed	Maximum unsigned
TINYINT	1	-128	127	255
SMALLINT	2	-32768	32767	65535
MEDIUMINT	3	-8388608	8388607	16777215
INT	4	-2147483648	2147483647	4294967295
BIGINT	8	-2^{63}	$2^{63}-1$	$2^{64}-1$

In each table, one integer field may have the optional property *AUTO_INCREMENT*. When used, this provides a primary key for the table. This property may only be used on an integer, and only once per table. It allows rows to be uniquely identified.

MySQL supports two floating point types: FLOAT and DOUBLE. These are stored as an approximate value; because of the nature of floating point numbers, they do not represent a number exactly. There is limited use for values that are not exact; as such, they warrant little more than a passing mention here.

MySQL supports an exact-value fixed-point type: DECIMAL. When using a DECIMAL type, the number of digits before and after the decimal point are explicitly stated. A DECIMAL column is declared with two parameters, such as *DECIMAL(4,2)*. The first number indicates the *total* number of digits the column may use, and the second number indicates how many of those digits belong after the decimal point. Because the DECIMAL data type is stored exactly, it is suitable for use with currency. For example, in a table storing information about different tax rates, we might declare the column as *DECIMAL(3,2)*, as Tennessee has the highest tax rate at 9.45 percent, for which we would need three digits, two of them after the decimal point. (Or if we expect that to increase, we might declare it as *DECIMAL(4,2)*, in the event that the rate jumped above 10 percent.) Or if using very large numbers, such as storing the yearly revenue of Walmart, we might use *DECIMAL(14,2)* to store *485873914829.15*, which on output we would format as $485,873,914,289.15. The DECI-MAL type can store a maximum of 65 digits.

STRING DATA TYPES

MySQL offers myriad data types for storing strings. Each offers different advantages and changes the way string data is stored and retrieved. String types can be used for storing both textual data and binary data.

CHAR

CHAR is used to store textual data, ideally of a fixed length. A column would be declared as CHAR(5), which indicates a field five characters long. CHAR always stores the data using the same number of bytes, even if the data is shorter. When storing a value, CHAR pads with spaces on the right; trailing spaces are removed when retrieving the value.

VARCHAR

VARCHAR is also used to store textual data, with two important differences. First, trailing spaces are preserved when data is stored and retrieved. Second, it uses a variable amount of space equal to the length of the string plus one byte. As most text is of variable length, especially when entered by a user, VARCHAR is most often the appropriate text column to use. When defining a column as VARCHAR, the maximum number of characters is specified. A column declared as VARCHAR(250), for example, can store up to 250 characters and use at most 251 bytes per row (but will use less for shorter strings).

BINARY and VARBINARY

BINARY and VARBINARY act much like CHAR and VARCHAR, except that they are treated as strings of bytes, rather than strings of characters. BINARY fields are padded with null characters, not spaces. "A" and "a" are different values because the underlying byte values are different; whereas in CHAR and VARCHAR, they are equal. Sizes specified for BINARY and VARBINARY specify the size in bytes, not characters. These fields are most appropriate for storing binary file data.

BLOB and TEXT

The BLOB and TEXT types are used to store large amounts of binary and textual data, respectively. While a standard MySQL row has a maximum size of 64KB, these types of fields are stored differently, allowing the limit to be circumvented. They are each available in four sizes: TINYTEXT stores text with a maximum length of 256 (2^8). TEXT stores up to 65,536 (2^{16}) characters. MEDIUMTEXT stores 2^{24} characters (about 16.7 million), and LONGTEXT stores 2^{32} characters (over 4.3 billion). TINYBLOB, BLOB, MEDIUMBLOB, and LONGBLOB have the same limitations, but act as binary strings. As these field types are stored differently, there is a performance hit when using them, so they should be avoided if there is a more suitable field type.

ENUM

An ENUM field is an enumerated list. This field type should be used for columns in which there are a set number of textual values. ENUM is a little special, for the following reasons:

- The field is defined as having a set of values. ENUM fields can be specified with up to 65,536 different values although the MySQL documentation specifies a "practical limit" of 3,000.
- The values stored require much less space to store. The values themselves are stored as part of the table definition, and the rows only store an index number. This can save a great deal of space on a large table.
- Values that are not in the column's definition may not be inserted, and an empty string or NULL is stored instead.
- ENUM values, when sorting, sort in the order listed in the column definition. This can be used to provide a custom sorting order for a set of values.

An example of an ENUM column might be storing the full names of states in a table containing a list of all zip codes in the United States. The zip code would be stored as CHAR(5). The city would be defined as a VARCHAR of however long the longest city name we can find is. The state abbreviation would be CHAR(2), and the full state name could be stored on the table as an ENUM field. (It could also be stored separately as a lookup table, but it may be more performant to store it on the same table.)

SET

A SET field acts like an ENUM field that can contain multiple values. These values, when stored and retrieved, are separated by commas, so the values themselves should not contain commas. They cannot contain more than 64 values in the field definition.

DATE DATA TYPES

MySQL offers several different date and time formats, each with their own advantages. These types, obviously, are appropriate for storing dates, times, and durations.

DATE

The DATE type should be used to denote a day. No time is stored in a DATE field. Dates may be in the range from *1000-01-01* to *9999-12-31*. A special "zero" value of *0000-00-00* is also allowed. DATE permits partial dates as well; *2018-04-00* may be used to denote April 2018.

DATETIME

The DATETIME field specifies both a date and a time in the same field. Generally, it should be used instead of separate DATE and TIME fields. It covers the same span of time as DATE: *1000-01-01 00:00:00* to *9999-12-31 23:59:59*. As with DATE, the month and day, and additionally any part of the time value, may be zero or a valid value for the date as a whole. DATETIME is generally the most appropriate for field type to store a date and time value.

TIMESTAMP

The TIMESTAMP column stores dates in a manner similar to a traditional UNIX timestamp, as the number of seconds since the start of the UNIX Epoch. As such, TIMESTAMP only has a valid range from *1970-01-01 00:00:01* to *2038-01-19 03:14:07*, when the number of seconds exceeds what can be stored in a 32-bit integer. However, storing a value in a TIME-STAMP column may be easier when working with many users across different time zones; the desired time zone may be specified in the connection, and MySQL will automatically convert values stored and retrieved as needed (which does not happen with DATETIME values). Although

TIMESTAMP values can be stored and retrieved in standard date and time formats, this conversion may be bypassed by using FROM_UNIXTIME() to insert and UNIX_TIMESTAMP() to retrieve values without performing conversion.

TIME

The TIME type stores a time only, without regard for a date. Because of this, it is most suited to storing a *duration*, rather than a moment in time. It can store a range of time between "-838:59:59" and "838:59:59"; that is, one second less than 839 hours in either direction. An appropriate use of the TIME type would be to store how fast runners complete a race.

THE SPECIAL VALUE *NULL*

Note: In this section, we refer to both NULL and *NULL*. NULL (without italics) is used to indicate a property of a field. *NULL* (with italics) is used to indicate the value.

There is a value in MySQL unlike any other: *NULL*. Any field may be defined as either NULL or NOT NULL, and when defined as NOT NULL, this value is not allowed. It is important to understand what *NULL* is and is not and how to use it.

NULL represents "no data." Specifically, it represents a lack of data. In a numeric column defined as NULL, a value of 0 is allowed. This is different from *NULL*. In a VARCHAR column, an empty string (") is allowed. This is different from *NULL*.

NULL is a value that is not equal to anything, *including itself*. Comparing *NULL* to any value will result in the expression evaluating to *NULL*, and *NULL* is not true. To test if a value is null, "IS NULL" is used instead.

In a phpMyAdmin window, try running the following query:

```
SELECT 1 = 1, 1 = 0, 1 = NULL, 0 = NULL,
    '' = NULL, NULL = NULL, NULL != NULL,
    NULL IS NULL
```

You should see the following results (Figure 3.3):

+ Options

1 = 1	1 = 0	1 = NULL	0 = NULL	" = NULL	NULL = NULL	NULL != NULL	NULL IS NULL
1	0	NULL	NULL	NULL	NULL	NULL	1

Figure 3.3. Desc: Comparisons involving *NULL*

See what MySQL returns for various comparisons. Does 1 equal 1? Yes, so the first column contains a 1, which MySQL uses to represent true. Does 1 = 0? No, so the second column contains a 0, used to represent false. Does 1 = *NULL*? The answer is *NULL*. This isn't quite the same as a false answer, as shown in the next column, when we ask if 0 = *NULL*. See also that *NULL* is not equal to the empty string, it is not equal to itself, and it is not *not* equal to itself. However, it is true that *NULL* is *NULL*.

So why does such a value exist? It makes it easier to work with certain sets and types of data. *NULL* values are ignored when working with aggregate functions. There will be more on these later, but for now, consider a table in which is stored the annual salary of survey respondents, rounded to the nearest $1000, and stored in a numeric column named *salary*. If a respondent chooses not to answer the question, *NULL* is stored, not zero. Then it is possible to determine the minimum salary using MIN(salary), the maximum salary using MAX(salary), and the average salary using AVG(salary). Each of these calculations ignores the *NULL* values stored when users chose not to answer the question, whereas a value of zero would affect both the minimum and average calculations.

MYSQL STATEMENTS

The basic "unit of operation" of MySQL is the statement. A statement, also called a query, is a specially formatted command that tells MySQL to perform a particular operation. Statements can be logically grouped into different categories. Data definition statements define or change the structure of tables, databases, and other aspects of the MySQL setup. To save space, this book largely skips discussion of these statements. Their functions are performed via phpMyAdmin in the project section. This book also skips discussion of statements relating to transactions, replication, and database administration because these are a higher level than the target audience.

This book instead focuses on the bread and butter of MySQL statements: data manipulation statements. And even then, only the four most useful: INSERT, SELECT, UPDATE, and DELETE.

To start, create an example table. The "test" database may already exist on your system. If it does not, create it, then create a table as shown below. The table name used here is *employees* (Figure 3.4).

Name	Type	Length/Values	Default	Collation	Attributes	Null	Index	A_I	Comments
id Pick from Central Columns	MEDIUMINT		None				PRIMARY PRIMARY		
fname Pick from Central Columns	VARCHAR	15	None				---		
lname Pick from Central Columns	VARCHAR	15	None				---		
hire_date Pick from Central Columns	DATE		None				---		
salary Pick from Central Columns	DECIMAL	8,2	None		UNSIGNE		---		
job Pick from Central Columns	ENUM	'CEO','Manager','Gru Edit ENUM/SET values	As defined: Grunt				---		
last_modified Pick from Central Columns	DATETIME		CURRENT_TIMEl		on update		---		

Figure 3.4. Desc: Creating the employees table

In our sample employees table, we have an *id* field, a MEDIUMINT with the AUTO_INCREMENT attribute set (A_I), defined as the primary key. *fname* and *lname* are varchar(15) columns for first and last name. The date of hire is stored as a DATE field named hire_date. The salary is DEC-IMAL(8,2), which allows values up to 999,999.99. Apparently, nobody will make $1 million per year. *job* is an ENUM which can be one of the values "Grunt", "Manager", or "CEO", with a default of "Grunt". Thanks to the order, we have defined that CEO > Manager > Grunt. Finally, a *last_modified* column of type DATETIME exists, with a default value of CURRENT_TIMESTAMP and the attribute ON UPDATE CURRENT_ TIMESTAMP specified, so whenever a row is created or edited, this field is set to when it occurred. There are additional fields to the right of the ones displayed, but they are not used in this example and are beyond the scope of this book.

INSERT

The INSERT statement is used to add rows to a table. It has two main forms:

```
INSERT INTO table (field list) VALUES (value
    list)
INSERT INTO table SET field1 = value1,
    field2 = value2...
```

Which version you use is up to you. Add some rows to the table using the SQL tab and the INSERT statement. Multiple statements can be run at the same time by separating them with a semicolon, as follows:

```
INSERT INTO employees (fname, lname, hire_date,
    salary, job) VALUES ('Mike', 'Smith', '2017-
    02-24', 750000, 'CEO');
INSERT INTO employees SET fname='John',
    lname='Parker', hire_date='2018-01-15',
    salary='35500.25', job='Manager';
INSERT INTO employees (hire_date, salary,
    fname, lname) VALUES ('2017-09-30',
    25575.20, 'Clark', 'Gabor'), (20170630,
    27500, 'Peter', 'Holmes');
```

After running the above queries, click the Browse tab in phpMyAdmin to see the data saved. Note that we did not specify the *id* for any row, as is typical for an auto-increment column, so the rows are numbered sequentially. MySQL also accepted dates as either a string, such as *'2018-01-15'*, or a numeric value, as in Peter's *20170630*. Every row received the same default value for *last_modified*, the time the query ran, and when the *job* was not specified, it used the default value of *'Grunt'*. MySQL also understood both a numeric value and a string value for salary, and converted it appropriately.

While INSERT statements only operate on a single table at once, other statements can use multiple tables. Before moving on, create another table called *phone_numbers*, and give it the following four fields: *id*, a MEDIUMINT field with AUTO_INCREMENT set as the PRIMARY KEY; *employee*, another MEDIUMINT field; *type*, an ENUM field with the options *Cell*, *Home*, and *Work*; and *number*, a CHAR(10) field. This can also be done with the following query, run on the *test* database.

```
CREATE TABLE phone_numbers (
    id MEDIUMINT NOT NULL AUTO_INCREMENT,
    employee MEDIUMINT NOT NULL,
    type ENUM('Cell','Home','Work') NOT NULL,
    number CHAR(10) NOT NULL,
    PRIMARY KEY (id)
);
```

Then, insert the following values. Either run the below query or use phpMyAdmin.

```
INSERT INTO phone_numbers (employee, type,
    number) VALUES
(1, 'Cell', '9145551631'),
(1, 'Work', '9805551346'),
(1, 'Home', '9145553123'),
(2, 'Work', '9805551560'),
(3, 'Work', '9805551439')
```

Now that there are two tables, let's examine the other types of queries.

SELECT

The SELECT statement is the most common type of query run against a database. It is used to retrieve stored values. You have likely already seen it in phpMyAdmin in its simplest form; for example, SELECT * FROM employees retrieves all values from the employees table. The most complicated select query—that we'll be looking at, anyway—looks like this:

```
SELECT [DISTINCT] field_list
FROM table_list
WHERE where_conditions
GROUP BY expressions
HAVING where_conditions
ORDER BY expressions [DESC]
LIMIT number(s)
```

Well now. Time to break that down a little.

The SELECT clause specifies what is to be selected. It is a list of fields from the list of tables. As a shortcut, an asterisk (*) can be used to specify all fields. If a field is not ambiguous, the field name may be used alone. If more than one field has the same name, use the table name as well to specify which field to select. Any field may be aliased using the AS keyword. If tables *table1* and *table2* both contain a field called *date*, then they could both be selected using SELECT t1.date AS date1, t2.date AS date2. If the query would result in multiple identical rows, using SELECT DISTINCT can filter out duplicates.

The FROM clause specifies which tables to select from. These too can be aliased. Multiple tables are joined together in one of four ways: A CROSS JOIN includes all rows from all tables in every combination, an INNER JOIN only includes rows when both tables match a specified condition, a LEFT JOIN includes all rows from the table on the left and any matching rows from the table on the right, and a RIGHT JOIN includes all rows from the table on the right and any matching rows from the table on the left. For CROSS, LEFT, and RIGHT JOINs, if a table has no matching rows, its fields in the result set are filled with NULLs. Each of these, except the CROSS JOIN, specifies how the tables are to be joined using an ON clause. Try each of the following queries below to see the results. (Run them separately.) Note that in MySQL, testing whether something is equal uses a single equals sign. This is standard for SQL languages, but it's different from other languages in which it may not be clear from context whether the operation is testing equality or assigning a value.

```
SELECT * FROM employees CROSS JOIN phone_
    numbers;
SELECT * FROM employees INNER JOIN phone_
    numbers ON employees.id = phone_numbers.
    employee;
SELECT * FROM employees AS e LEFT JOIN phone_
    numbers AS pn ON e.id=pn.employee;
SELECT * FROM employees AS e RIGHT JOIN phone_
    numbers AS pn ON e.id=pn.employee;
```

Of the four queries, the cross join is least useful in actual use. The inner join would be useful if we needed a list of phone numbers for employees. The left join would be used if we needed a list of employees, with or without phone numbers. The right join would help us find phone numbers for which there is no matching employee.

Joins are not limited to matching on equality. SELECT * FROM employees INNER JOIN phone_numbers ON employees.id > phone_numbers.employee is a perfectly valid MySQL query, even if the result makes no sense.

There is also another way to specify how to join the tables: with USING. When joining two tables, if the tables are to be joined such that two identically named fields are equal, USING may be used instead. For example, SELECT * FROM employees INNER JOIN phone_numbers USING (id) would join the *employee* table with the *phone_numbers* table wherever the *id* columns are equal. In this case, that would not be useful, but if both the employee.id and *phone_numbers.employee* fields were named *employee_id*, then the query could be written as SELECT * FROM employees INNER

JOIN phone_numbers USING (employee_id). This may be something to keep in mind when deciding field names for your database.

The WHERE clause is used to filter the rows of the tables used. It's not often that the entirety of a table is needed all at once. Say, for example, a list of all managers' phone numbers is needed. Using the tables above, SELECT * FROM employees AS e INNER JOIN phone_numbers AS pn ON e.id=pn.employee WHERE e.job='Manager' would return rows where the employee's job is "Manager."

The WHERE clause can also be used with LEFT or RIGHT JOINs to find data in one table that is missing in another table. SELECT * FROM employees AS e INNER JOIN phone_numbers AS pn ON e.id=pn.employee WHERE pn.number IS NULL will select all employees who do not have any phone numbers stored. (Recall that IS NULL must be used to test whether something is null. WHERE pn.number = NULL will not work.) Because there is no matching row selected from phone_numbers, any field could be used in the WHERE clause. WHERE pn.id IS NULL would work just as well.

The GROUP BY clause is used along with aggregate functions. (More on those coming up.) One common aggregate function is COUNT(). COUNT() simply counts the number of non-*NULL* values of a field. It does not count the number of distinct values unless specified. Try the queries below, one at a time:

```
SELECT COUNT(type) FROM phone_numbers;
SELECT COUNT(DISTINCT type) FROM phone_
    numbers;
SELECT e.fname, e.lname, COUNT(number) FROM
    employees AS e LEFT JOIN phone_numbers AS
    pn ON e.id=pn.employee GROUP BY e.id;
```

The first query counts all rows with a non-*NULL* value. That's all five of them. The second counts the number of different value, which is three. The third query groups the rows by the *id* field in the *employee* table and counts the non-*NULL* values for each group. In Peter's case, that number is zero.

It's important to mention in the example above that the query groups by e.id, but it selects fields (*e.fname* and *e.lname*) that are not part of the GROUP BY. This is not allowed in other flavors of SQL, but MySQL tolerates it. However, when doing this, there is no guarantee which field that is not part of the GROUP BY is returned. In this particular case, this doesn't matter; *fname* and *lname* are from the same row as *id* in the *employees* table. However, SELECT type, number FROM phone_numbers GROUP BY type is perfectly valid MySQL, and the number returned for each type (or, at least with this data, the "Work" type) is not guaranteed to be any particular value. Note that MySQL can be configured so that any field in the SELECT clause must either be an aggregate function or part of the GROUP BY; if the last query in the block failed, try GROUP BY fname, lname instead.

The HAVING clause functions much like the WHERE clause does, but it acts on the result set after any GROUP BY operations. Take a look at the following two queries and try to figure out what they accomplish before running them:

```
SELECT fname, lname, COUNT(number) AS numbers
    FROM employees AS e LEFT JOIN phone_
    numbers AS pn ON e.id=pn.employee WHERE
    type!="Work" GROUP BY fname, lname HAVING
    numbers = 0;

SELECT fname, lname COUNT(number) AS numbers
    FROM employees AS e INNER JOIN phone_
    numbers AS pn ON e.id=pn.employee WHERE
    type='Work' GROUP BY fname, lname HAVING
    numbers > 1;
```

The first query returns a list of all employees who do not have any nonwork phone numbers. The second query returns a list of employees who have more than one work phone number.

The ORDER BY clause specifies how to order the result set. When records are inserted into tables, MySQL generally returns them in the order inserted. However, after deleting records and adding new ones, this is no longer the case, and it's likely that the result should be sorted based on something other than the order the rows were inserted. Below, the first query shows a list of employees, sorted by last name, then first name. The second query shows a list of our newest employees first. If multiple employees had the same hire date, the name would break the tie. Note that by default, values sort in ascending order. DESC may be specified after each field, which should sort in descending order instead.

```
SELECT * FROM employees ORDER BY lname, fname;
SELECT * FROM employees ORDER BY hire_date
    DESC, lname, fname;
```

Finally, the LIMIT clause, as expected, limits the result to the number of rows given. The LIMIT clause is applied after all other clauses, including GROUP BY and ORDER BY. This query would determine the last hired employee.

```
SELECT * FROM employees ORDER BY hide_date DESC
    LIMIT 1;
```

As tables grow, LIMIT becomes more important when dealing with results that may have an excessively large number of rows, and the results might be displayed on multiple pages. LIMIT can be used to specify a starting row, as well, with the first row starting at zero. A comma separates the starting row from the desired row count in the result. Therefore, LIMIT 1 is equivalent to LIMIT 0, 1. A typical LIMIT clause might contain 50 results, such that a second page of results would have LIMIT 50, 50 at the end, but our *employees* table has only four rows. SELECT * FROM employees ORDER BY hire_date DESC LIMIT 3,1 would select the third most recently hired employee.

UPDATE

The UPDATE statement is used to change existing rows in a table. It can affect either a single table or multiple tables.

```
UPDATE tables
SET assignments
WHERE where_conditions
ORDER BY expressions
LIMIT number
```

Note that ORDER BY and LIMIT are only allowed when working with a single table. Using UPDATE is fairly straightforward compared to SELECT. For example, in the example *employees* table, we can change Peter Holmes to a Manager as follows:

```
UPDATE employees SET job = 'Manager' WHERE
    id = 4
```

And to update John Parker's work number, this would work:

```
UPDATE employees, phone_numbers SET number =
    '9805554569' WHERE employees.id = phone_
    numbers.employee AND employees.fname =
    'John' AND employees.lname = 'Parker'
```

This example, of course, is rather contrived. It would be easier to use the id of John's record in the *employees* table and simply update the *phone_numbers* table WHERE employee = 2.

DELETE

Rounding out the pack is the DELETE statement. The DELETE statement is used to remove rows from a table. It also has a single table syntax and a multiple table syntax.

Single table:

```
DELETE FROM table
WHERE where_condition
ORDER BY expressions
LIMIT number
```

As with UPDATE, the ORDER BY and LIMIT clauses are only available in the single table syntax. ORDER BY is only useful when LIMIT is also specified because DELETE will delete all matching rows. In the example *phone_numbers* table, we might decide we no longer want to store cell phone numbers:

```
DELETE FROM phone_numbers WHERE type = 'Cell'
```

The multiple table syntax can be used one of two different ways:

```
DELETE tables_to_delete_from
FROM tables_to_examine
WHERE where_conditions
```

or

```
DELETE FROM tables_to_delete_from
USING tables_to_examine
WHERE where_conditions
```

It turns out John Parker isn't a very good manager, and so we fired him from the company. Both his phone numbers and his employee record are getting deleted.

```
DELETE employees, phone_numbers FROM employees,
    phone_numbers WHERE employees.id = 2 AND
    employees.id = phone_numbers.employee
```

is equivalent to

```
DELETE FROM employees, phone_numbers USING
    employees, phone_numbers WHERE employees.
    id = 2 AND employees.id = phone_numbers.
    employee
```

It is not necessary to delete the rows from all tables examined. For example, the following query could be used to delete the phone numbers of all Grunts:

```
DELETE phone_numbers FROM employees, phone_
    numbers WHERE employees.job = 'Grunt' AND
    employees.id = phone_numbers.employee
```

INDEXES

When a table is small, it's fast. MySQL can very quickly determine whether a table has a row where a field has a certain value when the table only has four rows (and therefore, only four values to check). Tables in MySQL, however, can become very, very large. As a table grows, checking a field for a particular value increases, so while a table with four rows is always fast, a table with four million rows might not be. And worse, if that four-million-row table needs to be joined to itself, well, come back tomorrow to see if the query has finished running. Even when a table has four million rows, however, odds are not all of them are interesting. Perhaps only four—or more likely, one—of the four million are relevant to our interests. Here is where indexes help.

An index can be created on one or more fields in a table. It keeps track of the values for the field and the rows in the table that correspond to those values in such a way that it drastically increases the speed of a query that uses it. MySQL offers three types of indexes that are covered here:

An index of type *INDEX* is simply that: An index is created of the values in the field and the rows they point to, allowing for fast look up of table rows.

A *UNIQUE* index requires that no value in the index is equal to another; that is, two rows cannot be equal in the fields that are part of a *UNIQUE* index. Note carefully the wording here! Recall that *NULL* is not equal to *NULL*; therefore, it is perfectly acceptable to have two *NULL* values in a "*UNIQUE*" index! When a *UNIQUE* index exists, attempting to add another row with the same values as a row already in the index will cause the query to fail.

A *PRIMARY* index requires that all values (or for multiple fields, sets of values) are distinct, and additionally, all columns in a *PRIMARY* key must be NOT NULL. Primary keys are often an AUTO INCREMENT column; neither can be *NULL*, and both must be unique. However, while an AUTO INCREMENT column must be part of an index, it need not be a *PRIMARY* index; likewise, a *PRIMARY* index may exist on a table with no AUTO INCREMENT column.

While indexes do an excellent job of increasing the speed of queries, they do have two downsides. One, additional space is needed beyond what is required for the table data. It is possible for an index to use more space than the table itself, especially if the table has few fields. Two, whenever a row is inserted, performance suffers (very) slightly, as the row must be added to the index. In practice, however, a table of substantial size which is read from (not only written to) will require one or more indexes.

As a rule, you should create an index for one of two reasons: either to enforce unique values on a field or set of fields, or whenever a field is often used to find rows. At first thought, it might seem that creating an index to enforce unique values is unnecessary. After all, it's easy enough to check whether an existing row has those values before trying to insert a row. There are two issues with that approach, however. First, another user or connection could insert a row with those values between the time you check and the time you insert (unless you do it all in one query, which is possible). Second, if it's necessary to look up a row by a field or set of fields, well . . . that's what an index helps with anyway.

Let's take a closer look at the second reason: MySQL uses an index to find rows in a table. This encompasses several different cases. If the *phone_numbers* table from the previous section had an index on the *employee* field, not only would the index be used for a SELECT statement, such as SELECT * FROM phone_numbers WHERE employee = 3, it would also be used in UPDATE or DELETE statements, such as UPDATE phone_numbers SET number='9485551304' WHERE employee = 3 AND type='Work' or DELETE FROM phone_numbers WHERE employee = 3. It would also use it on a table join, such as SELECT * FROM employees INNER JOIN phone_numbers ON employees.id = phone_numbers.employee. MySQL, however, has some limitations on when it will use an index:

- In each query, MySQL can only use one index per table. It will try to use the most appropriate one.
- For an index with more than one field, it must use the fields in order. If an index is created on both the *employee* and *type* fields in the *phone_numbers* table, then a query such as SELECT * FROM phone_numbers WHERE type = 'Cell' would not use that index, because without using the first part of the index—the *employee* value—it would have to search the entire index. However, running the query SELECT * FROM phone_numbers WHERE employee = 3 would be able to use the index, as the first part of the index is the *employee* field, and the *type* field would be ignored.
- The index must be used by all conditions that are joined by *OR*. For example, if an index exists on the *employee* and *type* fields in the *phone_numbers* table, a query such as SELECT * FROM phone_numbers WHERE employee = 3 OR number = '9805558143' would not be able to use the index, as the index has no information about the contents of the *number* field, so MySQL must check every table row in case it matches that condition. MySQL *can* use the index if all parts joined by *OR* can use the index. Therefore, if the query is SELECT * FROM phone_numbers WHERE employee = 3 OR employee = 2, then because both parts can use the same index, MySQL can use it for the query.
- If MySQL determines that using the index would be slower than doing a full table scan, it will ignore the index.

OPERATORS AND FUNCTIONS

Most of MySQL's operators function similarly to other SQL variants, though this is different from their behavior in most programming languages. Therefore, a brief rundown is in order:

- The equals sign (=) is used for both comparison and assignment. Context is used to determine its function. WHERE column = 'value' implies comparison; SET column = 'value' implies assignment.
- Not equals may be represented by either != or <>.

- The mathematical operators +, −, *, and/work only with numbers. Some languages use + for string concatenation. In MySQL, 'star' + 'man' is the same as 0 + 0, and the result is 0, not 'starman'.
- *LIKE* is a keyword operator used to compare strings. It is an equality test that allows wildcards. The underscore character (_) matches a single character; a percent sign (%) matches any number of characters. WHERE column LIKE 'appl%' matches rows where *column* contains "apple", "application", or "appliance", for example. *LIKE* searches will used indexes if the field is indexed and a wildcard is not at the start of the string.
- *BETWEEN* is another useful keyword operator, shorthand for >= AND <=. SELECT * FROM table WHERE id BETWEEN 5 AND 10 is equivalent to SELECT * FROM table WHERE id >= 5 AND id <= 10.
- *IN* is a keyword operator that evaluates to true if an expression is contained in a value list. SELECT * FROM table WHERE id IN (2.7,10) is equivalent to SELECT * FROM table WHERE id = 2 OR id = 7 OR id = 10. *IN* can use an index if the field is indexed as well. *NOT IN* is also available; WHERE id NOT IN (2,7,10) would be the reverse of the above.

MySQL also has a wealth of functions. As with most languages, parentheses surround the argument list of a function. Unlike most languages, there cannot be a space between the function name and the open parenthesis. SELECT COUNT(*) FROM table returns the number of rows in a table; SELECT COUNT (*) FROM table will result in a syntax error. Many functions can take an arbitrary number of arguments; when this is the case, it is possible to use field names to perform the function on a field with many rows in a table. The function reference takes up no small part of the MySQL documentation, but some of the most commonly used functions are highlighted here.

Common string functions:

- CONCAT(*string1, string2, . . .*) takes multiple strings and concatenates them into a single string. Arguments may be either a field or a literal. If any argument is not a string, it is converted to one. If any argument is NULL, the result is NULL. SELECT CONCAT('c', 'on', 'cat'); returns 'concat'
- CHAR_LENGTH(*string*) returns the number of *characters* in *string*. SELECT CHAR_LENGTH('length'); returns 6. LENGTH(*str*) is also available, which returns the length of a string in *bytes*. For a string containing multibyte characters, this would be a different number.

- LOCATE(*needle, haystack, [pos]*) searches a string for a substring and returns its position. If the string does not contain the searched-for string, it returns 0. The third parameter is optional and specifies a starting position to search. SELECT LOCATE('ram', 'caramel'); returns 3.
- LPAD(*string, length, padding*) and its counterpart RPAD() return *string*, padded on the left or right respectively, to *length* characters, filling in with *padding*. SELECT LPAD('35', 5, '0') returns '00035'.
- REPLACE(*string, from, to*) replaces all instances of *from* in *string* to *to*. SELECT REPLACE('BANANA', 'N', 'W') returns 'BAWAWA'.
- SUBSTRING(*string, start, length*) returns part of a string. Length is optional. *string* is returned, starting with character number *start*. That is, the first character is number 1. SUBSTRING(*string*, 1) returns the entire string. SELECT SUBSTRING('BANANA', 2, 4) returns 'ANAN'.

Common date functions:

- DATE_FORMAT(*date, format*) formats a date, time, or datetime. The date parameter is required, and it helps to remember that the parameter order follows the function name. The list of specifiers allowed in the *format* string is rather long and can be found as part of the MySQL documentation: https://dev.mysql.com/doc/refman/8.0/en/date-and-time-functions.html#function_date-format. As an example, SELECT DATE_FORMAT('2018-04-25 18:30:15', '%c/%e/%y %l:%i %p') returns '4/25/18 6:30 PM'.
- NOW() returns the MySQL server's current datetime.
- UNIX_TIMESTAMP(*date*) returns the Unix timestamp of the given date. If no date is given, it returns the current Unix timestamp. If used on a TIMESTAMP column, the column is returned directly.
- FROM_UNIXTIME(*timestamp*) is the opposite of UNIX_TIME-STAMP(). A timestamp is given, and it returns the datetime using the standard MySQL format, or a format (the same as DATE_FOR-MAT's) can be passed as the second parameter. The server's time zone is used for both of these functions.

Common aggregate functions:

- MIN(*expr*) and MAX(*expr*) return the minimum and maximum values of a given expression, respectively. The behavior is obvious for numbers. For dates, these return the earliest and latest dates. For strings, they return as the first and last words you would find in a dictionary.

- COUNT(*expr*) is usually used as COUNT(*), which returns all matching rows. For a simple SELECT COUNT(*) FROM *table*, the number of rows in the table is returned. Adding a WHERE clause returns the number of rows matching the clause. Adding a GROUP BY clause returns the number of rows matching that group. If a different expression is used, such as COUNT(*field*), the number of non-NULL values of that field is returned instead. Furthermore, COUNT(DISTINCT *field*) returns the number of distinct values contained in *field*.
- GROUP_CONCAT(*expr*) returns a string with all values of the group concatenated together. DISTINCT may also be specified, as well as an ORDER BY clause and a SEPARATOR. Put together, and referring to our *phone_numbers* table from earlier in this section, SELECT GROUP_CONCAT(DISTINCT type ORDER BY type DESC SEPARATOR ', ') FROM phone_numbers would return the string 'Work, Home, Cell'.

PROJECT

While most of the queries will come in the last section as we manipulate the data, we can lay out the structure of the database now. Keep in mind that a table is needed for each "thing" in our application. Users are a thing and will need a table. Style suggestions are a thing. Comments are another thing, as is user *votes*. That would seem to be everything. In total, our database will have four tables.

Create a new database name *styleguide* in phpMyAdmin.

The *users* table will have five fields for an ID, the username, password, first name, last name, and an admin flag. As we expect fewer than 256 users, TINYINT UNSIGNED is sufficient for the ID field, which will be the primary key. The password field should be CHAR(60), with a collation of *latin1_general_cs*, because the value stored there will be case sensitive and will not use any characters outside of the latin1 character set. The admin field need only be a BIT(1), and its default can be 0. The other three fields will be allotted 25 characters, with a UNIQUE index on the username. Create this in phpMyAdmin on your own or run the following SQL from within the *styleguide* database:

```
CREATE TABLE users (
    uid TINYINT UNSIGNED NOT NULL
        AUTO_INCREMENT,
    username VARCHAR(25) NOT NULL,
```

```
password CHAR(60) CHARACTER SET latin1
    COLLATE latin1_general_cs NOT NULL,
firstname VARCHAR(25) NOT NULL,
lastname VARCHAR(25) NOT NULL,
`admin` BIT(1) NOT NULL DEFAULT b'0'
PRIMARY KEY (uid), UNIQUE (username))
    ENGINE = InnoDB;
```

Next, we need a table for style suggestions. The table will store an ID, a category, a summary of the suggestion, a detailed description, its current status (*'Proposed'*, *'Accepted'*, or *'Rejected'*), the user who proposed it, the date and time it was proposed, and the date and time it was accepted or rejected. You can name these fields as you wish. One possibility is in the SQL below:

```
CREATE TABLE suggestions (
    sid SMALLINT UNSIGNED NOT NULL
        AUTO_INCREMENT,
    category
        ENUM('General','HTML','CSS','PHP','SQL')
        NOT NULL,
    summary VARCHAR(100) NOT NULL,
    description VARCHAR(3000) NOT NULL,
    status ENUM('Proposed','Accepted','
        Rejected') NOT NULL,
    uid TINYINT UNSIGNED NOT NULL
    COMMENT 'ID of the user who proposed this
        suggestion',
    date_proposed DATETIME NOT NULL DEFAULT
        CURRENT_TIMESTAMP,
    date_voted DATETIME NULL DEFAULT NULL,
    PRIMARY KEY (sid),
    INDEX (category),
    INDEX (status)
) ENGINE = InnoDB;
```

Note that we have created separate indexes on the *category* and *status* fields. These are the only two fields that a search for suggestions is likely to be based upon. In practice, no indexes may be necessary, because our style guide may never exceed more than a couple hundred suggestions, and a couple hundred rows may well be fast enough; they are included here as an example of best practice. Note that if we were to design a user profile, including all suggestions made by a user, we might consider indexing the *uid* field as well. *date_proposed* defaults to CURRENT_TIMESTAMP, so we don't need to include it in INSERT queries. And *date_voted*, used to indicate when the suggestion was approved or rejected via vote, can be *NULL*, as before a suggestion is voted on, no such date exists.

Next, we need a table for comments. Comments belong to a suggestion, so they will contain the suggestion ID. We also need to know who wrote them, what they said, and when they said it, so we know how to order the comments when they are displayed. We'll give the comments their own ID, as well. Maybe we won't use it now, but if we allow users to edit or delete comments, they would need a way to uniquely identify them.

```
CREATE TABLE comments (
    cid SMALLINT UNSIGNED NOT NULL
        AUTO_INCREMENT,
    sid SMALLINT UNSIGNED NOT NULL COMMENT
        'Suggestion id',
    uid TINYINT UNSIGNED NOT NULL COMMENT
        'User id',
    ctext VARCHAR(5000) NOT NULL,
    cdate DATETIME NOT NULL DEFAULT
        CURRENT_TIMESTAMP,
    PRIMARY KEY (cid),
    INDEX (sid)
) ENGINE = InnoDB;
```

This follows a familiar pattern. By now, you should be able to identify and understand the limitations this table entails. Also note that there is an index on the suggestion ID field, *sid*, as comments will be looked up per suggestion.

The last table required will store user votes. Obviously, both the user and the suggestion will need to be stored. As for the vote, there are several ways to store it. We could store a vote up and a vote down in separate fields. That would have the advantage of being able to get both scores in a simple, single query. Or we could store a Yes vote, or a No vote, or a nonvote as an ENUM. We can actually do both by using only a BIT. A Yes vote can be represented by a 1, a No vote by a 0, and a nonvote by the row simply not being there. We'll use a little bit of magic later to figure out if the suggestion has reached a 50 percent threshold.

```
CREATE TABLE user_votes (
  uid TINYINT UNSIGNED NOT NULL,
  sid SMALLINT UNSIGNED NOT NULL,
  vote BIT NOT NULL,
  PRIMARY KEY (uid, sid)
) ENGINE = InnoDB;
```

Note that, in our project, the tables with ID fields conveniently begin with different letters, and we only have three of them. This makes it easy to remember what each ID is for. In a larger project, or if there are several tables starting with the same letter, we would do something more typical, such as *user_id, userID, userId, IDuser*, or something similar. Take your pick. Also note that other conventions for field or table names, such as *userVotes*, *UserVotes*, or if you don't mind using backticks, `user votes` are also valid. Just be sure to stick to a convention. A single style, if you will. You might even design a guide to help you keep track of it all!

That wraps up table creation. In the next chapter, we'll put our tables to use and write the queries to interact with them.

FURTHER READING

The MySQL documentation has versions for MySQL 5.5, 5.6, 5.7, and the recently released 8.0 (Versions 6 and 7 were skipped) under the MySQL Server heading:

https://dev.mysql.com/doc/

Entity Relationship Diagrams are a handy tool to plan the data your application will store and to map it to SQL tables.

https://www.lucidchart.com/pages/er-diagrams

https://en.wikipedia.org/wiki/Entity–relationship_model

CHAPTER 4

PHP

The fourth and final chapter of this book deals with a true programming language: PHP. PHP originally stood for personal home page, which was its original function, but it was later changed to the recursive acronym PHP: Hypertext Preprocessor. PHP's role in building in web page is to process input and generate output. The input it receives is very often passed to a database—MySQL in our case—for permanent storage. While PHP can be used to produce many kinds of output, from text files to CSVs to PDFs and even images, when used in a web server context, its most common output is HTML, which is then sent to the user's browser.

WHY PHP?

More than any other chapter of the book, this one may be the most controversial. No doubt there's someone who has found this book, scanned the table of contents, and flipped directly to this section. PHP has endured some (justified) critique: The language is at times inconsistent and counterintuitive. Its built-in functions reflect the language's originally ad hoc growth. Very old string functions look like they have C-style names such as *strpos*, *stripos*, or *nl2br*. Newer functions may have names that are exceedingly long, such as *array_reverse* or *get_html_translation_table*. And don't try to chain the ternary operator *?:*.

That said, the language does have its advantages. Variables are easily identifiable. Implicit type casting comes in handy when nearly everything starts as a string. PHP is available on nearly every hosting provider. It works well with Apache and MySQL. It has built-in (or compilable) support for everything from dates to being an SSH client to SNMP to dynamically generating images. And, of course, it's free. Perhaps even more importantly, it's easy to pick up and learn, which makes it ideal for our purposes.

GETTING INTO PHP: BASIC SYNTAX

Begin by changing the file extension of the existing *index.html* file to
.php, thereby making the file name *index.php*. Now open the file in a web
browser. It looks exactly the same! What's the point? Well, there isn't any
PHP code in the file. There aren't any PHP *tags* in the file, and therefore,
everything in the file is simply output to the browser.

In order to tell the web server that we want to run PHP code, we en-
close it in tags. To begin a PHP code block, use the open tag <*?php*. To
end the PHP code and return to treating the file as output, end the code
with *?>*. Note that if the file ends while we are "in" PHP, the end tag is
optional; in fact, its use is discouraged by the PHP manual. Therefore, we
could rewrite our Hello World! page from the HTML chapter as follows:

```
<?php echo "Hello, world!";
```

PHP tags and code can be placed anywhere inside a file. They can be at
the start of the file. They can be between elements. They can be in the middle
of an HTML element. Because the file is processed by PHP before it is sent
to the browser, it can even be in the middle of an HTML string (e.g., <input
value="<?php echo 1; ?>"/> is equivalent to <input value="1"/>).

Once inside PHP code, white space is not significant, and statements
are delineated with a semicolon. Therefore, to slightly expand our Hello,
world! example:

```
<?php
echo "Hello, world!";
echo "\nIt's a beautiful day today!";
```

The \n in the string represents a newline. Keep in mind that, if you
view this from a web browser, the newline character becomes a space, as
the web browser treats it as HTML, and in HTML, newlines are simply
condensed into spaces.

VARIABLES IN PHP

Variables in PHP are easy to identify; they are always preceded by a dollar sign. In PHP, variables do not need to be declared; you can use them
without declaring them. If you use them without declaring them, they are
assigned a default value based on context (more on that shortly). Variables

come in four types: scalar, array, object, and resource. A variable name starts with a letter or underscore and may contain any number of letters, underscores, or numbers. The special variable *$this* is reserved. Aside from *$this*, any function or language construct word can be used; thanks to the dollar sign, PHP knows the difference between the variable *$function* and the keyword *function*. Resources are special variables returned by certain functions and used in other functions; they will not be used in our project, and nothing more need be said about them here. Let's examine the other types.

SCALAR

A scalar is a solitary value. It may be a string, or an integer, a floating point (decimal) number, a boolean, or *null*. After using a variable for a particular type of value, it may be reused as another type of value, including changing the variable from a scalar to an array or object. It is up to the programmer to keep track of the contents of a variable. Because of this, the following are all valid, even next to each other in the same script:

```php
$x = 1;
$x = 0.56;
$x = 'howdy';
$x = false;
$x = null;
```

ARRAY

An array contains a set of values. Arrays can be either numerically indexed or key-indexed, *even in the same array*. Array elements may be any type of variable including other arrays, objects, or resources. Arrays may therefore be multidimensional and of mixed types. Arrays may be declared with either square brackets *[]* or with the *array()* construct. We use the construct here to follow the example of the documentation. The following is a valid array.

```php
$arr = array(2, 4, 6, 8 => 'eight', 'ten' =>
    10, false, 'odds' => array(1, 3, 5, 7,
    'nine'));
```

Try putting that line into a file, then call *print_r($arr);* to get a print-able version of the array. There are a few things to notice here. First, see that the first three elements have numeric indexes beginning with 0. Then, the fourth element is given an explicit value, 8, which does *not* fill in 3 through 7. The fifth element has 'ten' as its key and *10* as its value. The sixth element has a numeric key of *9* because the last used numeric key was *8*, and a value of *false* (which is not printed with *print_r()*), and the last element is itself an array with the string key *odds*. (You may also use *var_dump($arr)* to get a "dump" of the variable, which will print the value *false* along with the true types of the values as they are internally stored.)

Individual elements of the array are accessed with square bracket notation. $arr[0] returns the value *2*, $arr['ten'] returns *10*, and $ar-r['odds'][4] returns the string *'nine'*.

Arrays are not a fixed size. Elements can be added to an array, either with an explicit key ($arr[5] = 'banana' or $arr['banana'] = 5;) or by letting PHP use the next numeric key automatically: $arr[] = 'next';. Note that when adding elements to an existing array, the element is always added at the end, even if this results in the numeric keys becoming out of order.

Note that the above array is provided as an example of what's possible with PHP's array syntax. However, for your sanity, you should avoid using arrays of mixed types until you fully understand them. Arrays using only numeric keys or only string keys are easier to understand.

OBJECT

Objects are instantiations of classes. They can combine both properties (values) and functions into a single variable. User-defined classes and objects are not needed in our simple project and therefore are outside the scope of this book, although we will be using the built-in class *mysqli* to access MySQL. Accessing properties and functions of an object is done with the single-arrow operator -> or a hyphen followed by a greater than sign.

```
$db = new mysqli('localhost', $user,
    $password);
$result = $db->query('SELECT * FROM users');
```

A NOTE ABOUT STRINGS

Strings in PHP, as with many languages, can be delineated with either single quotes or double quotes. *Unlike* other languages, single and double quotes behave *differently*. When using double quotes, PHP performs variable interpolation on strings and escape sequences. When using single quotes, it does not. So in a block of code such as this:

```
$num = 4; $fruit = 'bananas';
$s1 = "I have $num $fruit.\n";
$s2 = 'I have $num $fruit.\n';
echo $s1, $s2;
```

$s1 will be set to *I have 4 bananas.* with a newline at the end. *$s2* will be set to *I have $num $fruit.\n*, exactly as it appears.

If including an element of an array with a named key, omit the quotes around the key in this instance: echo "I have $totals[bananas] bananas.";. Alternatively, put braces around the entire expression: echo "I have {$totals['bananas']} bananas.";

OPERATORS

As explained above, PHP is a loosely typed language. A variable can be any given type at any given time, whether that is an array, a number, a string, or a boolean. PHP converts variables as needed to evaluate an expression in a process known as type juggling. Operators may best be understood based on the types of expressions they juggle to and result in.

ARITHMETIC

The arithmetic operators are +, −, *, /, %, and **, for addition, subtraction (and negation), multiplication, division, modulo, and exponentiation. They juggle their operands to integers or floats (except the modulo operator, which only uses integers) and result in either an integer or float. Note that divided integers may result in a float. 5/2 is 2.5, not 2.

STRING

The only string operator is the concatenation operator, a period (.). This operator juggles its operands to strings, so $x = 99; $y = 'balloons'; $z = $x. ' '. $y; would set $z equal to "99 balloons". This is one instance in which whitespace acts a little strange. $x = 5.2 will cause *$x* to be the floating point value *5.2*, whereas $x = 5 . 2 will cause *$x* to be the string *"52"*. $x = 5. 2 is simply a syntax error.

INCREMENT

PHP supports ++ and --. They work entirely as expected with integers, returning integers. They also work with strings. $x = 'A'; $x++ results in *$x* set to *'B'*. Upon reaching Z, the value increments to AA, much like columns in a spreadsheet.

ASSIGNMENT

A simple equals sign = is used to assign a value to a variable, as we have seen so far. $x = 4 sets *$x* to the integer value 4. Combination assignment operators are also allowed, so +=, -=, *=, /=, %=, and .= will add, subtract, multiply, divide, modulo, and concatenate the two operands and assign the result to the operand on the left side. $x = 4; $x += 3; results in *$x* set to 7.

COMPARISON

The operators ==, !=, <>, <, >, <=, and >= are all supported for comparison, representing equal, not equal, not equal (again), less than, greater than, less than or equal to, and greater than or equal to. Keep in mind that because of type juggling, you can end up with some interesting results. For example, 0 == 'string' and 10 == '10 bananas' are true because the strings are converted to a numbers.

Because of this, PHP also provides the identity comparison operators === and !== for identical and not identical. The two operands are identical if they are equal and of the same type. They are not identical if either the value or the type is not the same. So while 0 == '0', 0 == false, '0' == false, and 0 == null are all true, replacing any of those with an identity comparison operator, such as 0 === '0', would result in a false expression.

LOGICAL

Logical operators juggle to booleans with the following rules:

- Nonzero numbers are true. Zero is false.
- Nonempty strings are true, except for "0" and the empty string " ", which are false.
- *null* is false.
- Arrays with elements are true. Empty arrays are false.

The logical operators are ||, &&, !, and the words *and*, *or*, and *xor*. || and && are logical OR and logical AND, and ! is logical NOT. The words *and*, *or*, and *xor* are a much lower precedence than the symbols, allowing for some flexibility. Also, PHP's logical operators are short-circuit, meaning that operands are only evaluated as needed to determine the value of the entire expression. Consider the following code:

```
some_function() or print '!'; //line 1
$x = some_function() or print '!';  //line 2
$x = some_function() || print '!';  //line 3
$x = (some_function() || print '!');  //line 4
```

In line 1, *some_function()* is evaluated. If it returns a truthy value, the *or* doesn't evaluate the print statement, as the entire expression will be true because the left side is true. If *some_function()* returns false, then the right side must be evaluated to see if it's true (*print* always returns 1, so it will always be true). An exclamation mark is printed. In line 2, the value of *some_function()* is assigned to *$x*. If that value is truthy, then the print statement does not execute. If it is falsey, the print executes. This is because the *or* operator has a lower precedence than assignment. In line 3, *some_function()* is evaluated, and if false, *!* is printed. However, because || has a higher precedence than the assignment, *$x* will end up with the value *true*, either because *some_function()* evaluates to a truthy value, or because *print* will because it returns 1. Line 3 is logically equivalent to line 4, which uses parentheses to explicitly show the order in which the expressions execute.

In practice, the syntax in line 2 is commonly seen. Care must be taken not to use || when *or* is intended, as line 3 (and line 4) is logically different from line 2.

LANGUAGE CONSTRUCTS

Many of the language constructs in PHP are similar to other languages and should be recognizable to even the beginning programmer. As such, this chapter spends little time describing them, as their use is self-evident. The following examples are assumed to take place inside a PHP code block (between *<?php* and *?>*).

echo
> *echo* is used to output a value or set of values.

```php
echo "Hello, new user!";
echo "The value of x is ", $x;
```

print
> *print* is also used to output a value. Unlike *echo*, it cannot output multiple values separated by commas. However, *print* technically returns a value, so it can be used in instances such as this:

```php
$x >= 0 or print '$x is less than 0.';
```

if, else if, else

```php
if ($x > 0) {
    echo '$x is greater than 0.';
} else if ($x < 0) {
    echo '$x is less than 0.';
} else {
    echo '$x is equal to 0.';
}
```

while, do ... while

```php
$x = 1;
while ($x < 10) {
    echo "$x\n"; $x++;
}
$y = 1;
```

```
do {
    echo "$y\n"; $y++;
} while ($y < 10);
```

In a *do . . . while* loop, the conditional is at the end, so the loop always runs at least once.

for, foreach

While *for* is familiar, *foreach* may not be. *foreach* simply takes an array and iterates over it.

```
for ($x = 1; $x < 10; $x++) {
    echo "$x\n";
}
$array = array('Apples', 'Bananas',
    'Oranges');
foreach ($array as $key => $value) {
    echo "$key: $value\n";/* prints 0:Apples
        (with newline), etc. */
}
```

*switch (*and *case)*

In PHP, the switch expression matches the case if the two are *loosely equal*. That is, if they are ==, not necessarily ===. Furthermore, as in C, you can "fall through" from one case to the next. There is *not* an implicit break between cases; it must be specified. A *default* clause is also permitted.

```
$x = 'a';
switch ($x) {
    case 'b':
    case 'B':
        $y = 2;
        break;
    case 'a': case 'A':
        $y = 1; break;
    default:
        $y = 0;
}
```

include, include_once, require, require_once
> These four language constructs take a file's contents and treat them as if they were part of the current file at the location it occurs. Generally, these are used at the beginning of a file to include functions common to many scripts. By default, included files act like output; if the included files are to be executed as PHP code, they must have their own PHP tags inside them.
>
> *include* is used to include a file if it exists. If it does not, a warning is thrown, and script execution continues.
>
> *require* forces a file to be included. If it cannot, script execution halts.
>
> *include_once* and *require_once* act like *include* and *require,* but if the file in question has already been included, it is ignored. Generally, function declarations will use one of these *_once* constructs so as not to declare a function multiple times, which would result in an error.

FUNCTIONS

PHP has an enormous number of functions, far too many to completely cover in this book. Instead, this book will focus on the number of functions needed for the project: six. These functions, along with the mysqli extension discussed soon, are enough to understand the scripts that will finish up the project at the end of this chapter.

bool *empty(*var $var)
> *empty* takes a variable that may or may not be declared. If the variable is falsey—if it is undefined, *null, 0, ", '0', false,* or an array with no elements—it returns true. If the variable is defined and has some other value, *empty* returns false.

bool *isset(*var $var)
> *isset()* checks to see if a variable exists and is not *null,* returning true if that is the case, otherwise returning false.

string *htmlspecialchars(*string $string)
> Takes a string as a parameter and returns the string with special characters encoded as HTML entities such as < becoming <.

string *nl2br(*string $string)
> Takes a string as a parameter and returns the string with all newline characters ("\n") replaced with <br> tags. As we'll see later, this is used to keep newline characters in HTML output. Recall that a newline in HTML output condenses to a space. A generic version of this function can be found in *str_replace()*.

string *implode(*string *$glue*, array *$array)*

Takes an array (*$array*) and returns a string with the string *$glue* inserted between each element of the array. For example, implode(' :: ', array(1, 2, 3)) returns 1::2::3. There exists a corresponding function *explode* which does the opposite.

*header(*string *$string)*

Sends an HTML header. If this is used, it **must** be used before anything is output. For our project, we will use it to redirect the browser using relative paths, using the format header("Location: filename.php");. When performing such a redirection, the script should nearly always terminate; therefore, exit() should be called after the call to header().

string *password_hash(*string *$string*, int *$algo)*

This takes a string and an algorithm (in the form of a constant) and returns a hash (currently 60 characters) that can be checked with password_verify. According to the PHP documentation, using PASSWORD_DEFAULT as the second argument (*$algo*) is highly recommended.

bool *password_verify(*string *$password*, string *$hash)*

Given a *$password* and a *$hash* created by password_hash(), this returns true if the password is correct and false if the password is incorrect.

ADD YOUR OWN FUNCTIONS

To declare your own function in PHP, use the keyword function, give it a name, specify the parameters, and provide the function body.

```
$x = 10;
printFromZero($x);
function printFromZero($num, $step = 1) {
    for ($x = 0; $x <= $num; $x += $step) {
        echo "$x\n";
    }
}
```

Note that we set $x to the value 10, then pass it to the function as an argument. In the declaration, $step = 1 means that it's an optional argument. If it's passed, the passed value is used. If it's not provided, it defaults to the value 1. Also note that the variable $x contained inside the function is a *different* variable than the $x at global scope. In PHP, all variables are local to the function they are inside of unless the global keyword is used.

```php
$y = 10;
printY();
function printY() {
    global $y;
    print "$y\n";
}
```

This contrived example illustrates the behavior of global. Without that line, $y is undefined, and it would simply print a newline.

By default, PHP passes arguments by value. A copy is made of any parameters, and the function operates on the copy. It's also possible to pass by reference, in which the function operates on the original, by putting & before the parameter name:

```php
function addByValue($val) {
    echo "$val\n";
    $val = $val + 5;
    echo "$val\n";
}
function addByReference($ref) {
    echo "$ref\n";
    $ref += 5;
    echo "$ref\n";
}
$x = 10;
addByValue($x);
echo "$x\n";
addByReference($x);
echo "$x\n";
```

The above would print:

```
10   //Inside addByValue, before addition
15   //Inside addByValue, after addition
10   //After exiting addByValue
10   //Inside addByReference, before addition
```

```
15  //Inside addByReference, after addition
15  //After exiting addByReference
```

MY SQLi

PHP has a built-in extension for talking to MySQL: the *MySQLi* extension. (Well, it usually has it. If it doesn't, you may need to build your own or talk to your hosting provider.) The *MySQLi* extension has three primary classes: the *mysqli* class represents a connection to a MySQL server, the *mysqli_result* class represents the result of a query, and the *mysqli_stmt* class represents a prepared statement.

MYSQLi

While the *mysqli* class contains a wealth of functions and properties. Here are the most commonly used:

Constructor

Create a new *mysqli* object by instantiating the class. Pass it the host, MySQL username, password, and database name.

```
$mysql = new mysqli('localhost', 'myUser',
    'myPassword', 'test');
The $mysql object now represents a connection
    to the database.
```

Query()

Perform an SQL query. Once you have a connection, you can query the database. This function returns a *mysqli_result* object, or *FALSE* if the query fails. Because it returns false on failure, this is commonly paired with something to handle the case where it fails. Continuing from our *$mysql* variable created above, this would look like so:

```
$result = $mysql->query('SHOW TABLES') or
    exit('Error in query');
```

Error

If there is an error in your query, it will be stored as a string in this property.

```
$result = $mysql->query('SELECT * FROM
    table WHERE') or print 'Error in query: '.
    $mysql->error;
```

Affected_Rows

If the query is an *INSERT, UPDATE,* or *DELETE* query, this contains the number of rows affected by it.

```
$mysql->query('UPDATE table SET col = 4 WHERE
    col < 4');
echo $mysql->affected_rows. ' rows affected.';
```

MYSQLi_RESULT

After performing a *SELECT* query, mysqli->query() returns a *mysqli_result* object. The object does not contain the data itself but provides methods to retrieve it and some properties about it.

$num_rows

This contains the number of rows in the result set. Using the $mysql variable from above:

```
$result = $mysql->query("SELECT * FROM table
    LIMIT 50");
echo "There are ". $result->num_rows.
    " in the result set.";
```

fetch_row(), fetch_assoc(), and fetch_array()

Rows are fetched from the result using one of these methods. fetch_array() can take a parameter that allows it to act as either of the other two, but it's simpler just to use the other functions. fetch_row returns a row as a numbered array. fetch_assoc returns a row as a named array. fetch_array returns a row as both. If there are no more rows in the result set, these functions return *NULL* (which in PHP is a false value).

```
$result = $mysql->query("SELECT id, name FROM
    table WHERE id = 1 AND name = 'Tim'");
/* Method 1: fetch_row()
$row = $result->fetch_row(); */
//[0 => 1, 1 => 'Tim']
/* Method 2: fetch_assoc()
$assoc = $result->fetch_assoc(); */
//['id' => 1, 'name' => 'Tim']
/* Method 3: fetch_array()
$array = $result->fetch_array(); */
/* [0 => 1, 'id' => 1, 1 => 'Tim', 'name' =>
    'Tim'] */
```

In the example above, only one of the methods would work without including $result->data_seek(0); to reset the result pointer. These methods are not usually mixed. The result of each of these is shown above, if they were run separately. If they were run together without resetting the result pointer, $row would have the value above, and both $assoc and $array would be null. Because these functions return null when there are no more rows, they are commonly used in a loop:

```
while ($row = $result->fetch_assoc()) {
    print_r($row);
}
```

SQL INJECTION AND *MYSQLi_STMT*

Consider for a moment the following code.

```
$sql = new mysqli();
$query = "SELECT * FROM users WHERE
    username = '$username'";
$result = $sql->query($query);
```

A username is something that is provided by the user and supplied to your query. Seems straightforward, right? What if the user enters the value ' OR '1' = '1'? When inserted into the query, it becomes SELECT * FROM users WHERE username = " OR '1' = '1'. Because '1' is *always* equal to '1', this would always return every user. It might even do something more malicious; what if it were a *DELETE* query?

For this reason, **all data provided by a user must be sanitized**. Sanitizing user input simply means it is made safe to be part of a query. There are several ways to do this.

1. If the value should be a number, it can be cast in PHP. $id = (int)$id;
2. If the value only makes sense if it is one of a set of values, it can be checked to be sure it is identical to one, and not be used if it doesn't.
3. If the query will only be run a few times, the function *mysqli->real_escape_string()* can be used to make the string usable in a query, like so:

```
$sql = new mysqli();
$sanitized = $sql->escape_string($user_input);
$query = "SELECT * FROM table WHERE col =
    '$sanitized'";
$result = $sql->query($query);
```

If the query will be used many times, it's best to use a prepared statement.

MYSQLi_STMT

The *mysqli* extension allows the use of prepared statements. Follow these steps:

1. Use *mysqli->prepare()* to create the statement and receive a *mysqli_stmt* object.
2. Bind parameters using *mysqli_stmt->bind_param()*.
3. Execute the statement with *mysqli_stmt->execute()*.
4. Bind the result fields to variable using *mysqli_stmt->bind_result()*.
5. Store a row from the result to the variables in step 4 using *mysqli_stmt->fetch()*.

When preparing a statement, parameters are represented by unquoted question marks, and when calling *bind_param()*, the first parameter is a string containing the letters *i*, *d*, or *s*, depending on whether the variable is an integer, double, or string. In practice, it looks like this:

```
$sql = new mysqli();
$stmt = $sql->prepare("SELECT id FROM
    inventory WHERE type = ? AND price > ? AND
    category = ?");
$type = 4; $price = 12.50; $category =
    'games';
$stmt->bind_param('ids', $type, $price,
    $category);
$stmt->execute();
$stmt->bind_result($id);
$stmt->fetch();/* $id now contains the id of the
    first inventory item matching the search */
```

The *mysqli_stmt* class, like the *mysqli_result* class, also has properties such as *$affected_rows* and *$num_rows*. Note that to use *$num_rows*, you must first call *store_result()* so that the result is saved (see *guide.php* in the project at the end of this chapter).

THE FINAL PIECE: *$_POST* AND *$_GET*

At this point, you should know how to output HTML from PHP: simply echo or print it, or drop out of PHP using an end tag: ?>. You should know how to get data into and out of MySQL. There's just one piece left. How does data get *from* HTML *to* PHP?

Recall back in the HTML chapter of this book that HTML pages could have *forms*. Those forms were submitted using either a post or get method, and they could have input elements. Those input elements could have *names*. When the form is submitted, all the form information is stored in one of two variables: $_POST for forms submitted via the post method and $_GET for forms submitted via the get method. (In fact, anything after a question mark in the URL is submitted via get, it's possible for both variables to contain information!) $_POST and $_GET are arrays, and they're two of PHP's *superglobals*. A superglobal is a variable that is *automatically global* everywhere; therefore, it is available in all scopes including inside functions and included files. When the form is submitted, input elements are added to the array as array elements, as if they were being executed, as follows:

```
$_METHOD[<html_name>] = <html_value>
```

Consider the following HTML form:

```
<form action="save.php" method="post">
<input type="text" name="title"/>
<input type="checkbox" name="categories[]"
    value="1"/>
<input type="checkbox" name="categories[]"
    value="2"/>
<input type="submit"/>
</form>
```

When the form is submitted, the information will be put in the variable $_POST because the form uses the post method. $_POST will contain (at most) two elements: one has the key title and contains whatever the user entered into the text string. The other, if it exists at all, is a numeric array named categories. If the user didn't check either box, neither control was active, and therefore the array doesn't exist. If the user checked at least one, then $_POST['categories'] is a numeric array containing the values checked. (Note that the values are specified on the checkbox elements.) If the user were to type "Orange" into the text box and check both boxes above, then performing print_r($_POST) in *save.php* would result in this:

```
Array
(
    [title] => Orange
    [categories] => Array
    (
        [0] => 1
        [1] => 2
    )
)
```

AND ONE MORE THING: $_SESSION

Up until this point, everything that has existed in a PHP script has disappeared at the end of a page. Every connection to the database, every variable, all of it is lost when the script ends. (PHP does garbage collection on these. Don't worry about leaving database connections open.) However, once a user logs in, we need some way to track them.

PHP provides the superglobal variable $_SESSION to handle this. To use it, call session_start() in a script **before any output is sent to the browser**. Variables, such as a user's ID, can then be saved in the *$_SESSION* variable. They will be automatically available to other scripts as long as those scripts also call session_start() before sending any output. The user is given a PHP session ID, which is stored in their cookies. No data stored in $_SESSION is ever sent to the user using this method, and it lasts until the user closes their browser windows.

PROJECT

It's time to finish up the project using the existing styles and tables from the previous chapter. Start by opening index.php and change the links. One should read *Guide*, pointing to guide.php; one for *Suggestion Box*, pointing to suggestions.php; one to *Sign In*, taking the user to login.php; and in the admin section, one for *User List*, which goes to users.php. Then, move everything from the top of the file to the <div id="main"> tag to its own file, named header.php. We might not have any PHP code in it just yet, but we may change our minds.

header.php

```
<html>
<head>
<title>Pendity Software Style Guide</title>
<link rel="stylesheet" type="text/css"
    href="style.css"/>
</head>
<body>
<div id="icon"><img src="logo.png"/></div>
```

```
<div id="header">
<h1>Pendity Software</h1>
<h2>Style Guide</h2>
</div>
<div id="links">
<a href="guide.php">Guide</a>
<a href="suggestions.php">Suggestion Box</a>
<a href="login.php">Sign in</a>
<p>Admin Only:</p>
<a href="users.php">User List</a>
</div>
<div id="main">
```

Take the final three tags and move them to a new file named *footer. php*.

footer.php

```
</div>
</body>
</html>
```

The index file can then be changed to:

index.php

```
<?php require 'header.php'; ?>
<p>This is the page for the style guide.</p>
<?php require 'footer.php'; ?>
```

This allows us to use the same header and footer on every page. It saves typing, and it allows one file to be changed to change every page. Another task we will want to do often will be connecting to the database. When attempting the connection, we'll suppress any built-in warnings and simply exit with a generic message if anything goes wrong. In a more complicated system, we might log the error or provide more information, but this is simply an internal tool. In the script below, replace YOUR_MYSQL_USER and YOUR_MYSQL_PASSWORD with what they describe.

connect.php

```php
<?php
$db = @new mysqli('localhost', YOUR_MYSQL_
    USER, YOUR_MYSQL_PASSWORD, 'styleguide');
if (isset($db->connect_error)) {
    exit('An error occurred connecting to the
    database.');
}
?>
```

Our sign-in page will double as a sign-in and sign-up page, containing two forms that are handled by different scripts:

login.php

```php
<?php require 'header.php'; ?>
<div style="text-align: center">
<form action="dologin.php" method="post">
<p><b>Sign In:</b></p>
<p>Login<br/>
<input type="text" maxlength="25"
    name="username"/></p>
<p>Password<br/>
<input type="password" name="password"/></p>
<input type="submit" value="Log In"/>
</form>
</div>
<hr/>
<div style="text-align: center">
<p><b>Or create a new user:</b></p>
```

```html
<form action="newuser.php" method="post">
<table style="margin-left: auto; margin-right:
    auto;">
<tr><td>Username</td>
    <td><input type="text" maxlength="25"
    name="username"/></td></tr>
<tr><td>Password</td>
    <td><input type="password" maxlength="72"
    name="password"/></td></tr>
<tr><td>First Name</td>
    <td><input type="text" maxlength="25"
    name="firstname"/></td></tr>
<tr><td>Last Name</td>
    <td><input type="text" maxlength="25"
    name="lastname"/></td></tr>
</table>
<p><input type="submit" value="Create
    User"/></p>
</form>
</div>
<?php require 'footer.php'; ?>
```

Next, the script to handle user sign-ups. After including *connect.php*, we can use the $db variable to access the MySQL connection. Simply escape the data, save it, store it in the session to automatically log the user in, and redirect the user back to the index page.

newuser.php

```php
<?php
require 'connect.php';
$username = $db->escape_string(
    $_POST['username']);
$password = $db->escape_string(password_
    hash($_POST['password'], PASSWORD_DEFAULT));
$firstname = $db->escape_string(
    $_POST['firstname']);
```

```php
$lastname = $db->escape_string(
    $_POST['lastname']);
$query = "INSERT INTO users (username,
    password, firstname, lastname) VALUES
    ('$username', '$password', '$firstname',
    '$lastname')";
$result = $db->query($query);
if ($db->affected_rows == 1) {//insert was
    successful
        session_start();
        $_SESSION['userid'] = $db->insert_id;
        $_SESSION['name'] = $_POST['firstname'];
        header('Location: index.php');
} else {
    echo 'Your user account could not be
        created.';
}
```

At this point, you should be able to create a user for yourself, then use phpMyAdmin to change the admin flag to 1, indicating you are an admin. Next let's handle signing in with an existing account. Using the username provided, we retrieve the information. If the query fails, we give a generic error. If no row matches, the error is there is no user with that username. If the password fails, we say the password is incorrect. These error messages are more specific than you would normally find on a website open to the general public (generally, you would just say that the login attempt failed, not which part), but as an internal site, we take some liberties. Plus, we're not asking for an e-mail to allow the user to reset their information. Finally, if the password passes verification, we store the information in the $_SESSION array and redirect.

dologin.php

```php
<?php
require 'connect.php';
$username = $db->escape_string(
    $_POST['username']);
$query = "SELECT * FROM users WHERE
    username = '$username'";
```

```php
$result = $db->query($query);
if ($result === false) {
    require 'header.php';
    echo '<p>An error occurred when
    attempting to log in.</p>';
    require 'footer.php';
    exit();
}
if ($result->num_rows == 0) {
    require 'header.php';
    echo '<p>There is no user with that
        username.</p>';
    require 'footer.php';
    exit();
}
$row = $result->fetch_assoc();
if (password_verify($_POST['password'],
    $row['password'])) {
    session_start();
    $_SESSION['userid'] = $row['uid'];
    $_SESSION['name'] = $row['firstname'];
    header('Location: index.php');
    exit();
} else {
    require 'header.php';
    echo '<p>The password is incorrect.
        </p>';
    require 'footer.php';
}
```

Next, we want to make the user list. As part of this, we want to be sure the user is actually an administrator and allowed to see it. We might want to be able to check this elsewhere, too, so this is a good time for a function. We'll call it isAdmin(), and we'll pass it a user ID (called $uid in the function) to check. It will return true if the ID belongs to an admin, false otherwise.

isAdmin.php

```php
<?php
require_once 'connect.php';
```

```php
function isAdmin($uid) {
    global $db;
    $uid = (int)$uid;
    $query = "SELECT admin FROM users
            WHERE uid = $uid";
    $result = $db->query($query) or exit
            ("Error checking user for admin
            rights.");
    $row = $result->fetch_assoc();
    if ($row === false || $row['admin']
            == 0) {
    return false;
    }
    return true;
}
```

Now, we can use that and the user ID stored in our $_SESSION variable to find out if the current user is an admin. Note that if the user isn't even logged in, then $_SESSION['userid'] will be null, which the isAdmin() function turns into 0 when it casts it to an integer, and because there's no user with an ID of 0, it will return false anyway, which is what we want! The main point of the user list is to be able to delete users, so we provide a mechanism to do that via links.

users.php

```php
<?php
session_start();
require 'connect.php';
require_once 'isAdmin.php';
if (!isAdmin($_SESSION['userid'])) {
    header('Location: index.php');
    exit();
}
$query = "SELECT * FROM users";
$result = $db->query($query) or exit
    ("Error getting users.");
require 'header.php';
?>
<h1>User List</h1>
```

```
<table>
<tr><th>X</th><th>Username</th>
    <th>First Name</th><th>Last Name</th>
    <th>Admin</th></tr>
<?php
while ($row = $result->fetch_assoc()) {
    echo '<tr>';
    if ($row['uid'] == $_SESSION['userid']) {
    echo '<td></td>';
    } else {
    echo "<td><a class=\"delete\"
        href=\"deleteuser.
        php?uid=$row[uid]\">X</a></td>";
    }
    echo '<td>',
        htmlspecialchars($row['username']),
        '</td>',
    '<td>', htmlspecialchars(
        $row['firstname']), '</td>',
    '<td>', htmlspecialchars(
        $row['lastname']), '</td>',
    '<td>', $row['admin'], '</td></tr>';
}
?>
</table>
<?php
require 'footer.php';
```

Now for the delete script. We again make sure we're an admin, and then we delete the user with the user id found in the $_GET variable, as it was passed in as part of the URL. Just to be extra safe, we make sure we're not trying to delete ourselves. The exit() at the end of the file *is* superfluous, but it follows our rule of including it after a redirect via header().

deleteuser.php

```
<?php
session_start();
require 'connect.php';
require_once 'isAdmin.php';
```

```php
if (!isAdmin($_SESSION['userid'])) {
    header('Location: index.php');
    exit();
}
$uid = (int)$_GET['uid'];
$myid = (int)$_SESSION['userid'];
$query = "DELETE FROM users WHERE uid = $uid
    AND uid != $myid";
$result = $db->query($query);
if ($result === false) {
    require 'header.php';
    echo 'An error occurred trying to delete
    the user.';
    require 'footer.php';
}
header('Location: users.php');
```

Now that we have sessions and users working, we can revisit the header file to customize some of the links. If a user is signed in, there's no need to make them sign in again, so the "sign in" link can be changed to a "Welcome, <user>" link that isn't clickable. We also have a function to test whether someone is an admin, so we only need to show the admin section if they are. We can change header.php to what is shown below.

header.php

```php
<?php
session_start();
require_once 'isAdmin.php';
?><html>
<head>
<title>Pendity Software Style Guide</title>
<link rel="stylesheet" type="text/css"
    href="style.css"/>
</head>
<body>
<div id="icon"><img src="logo.png"/></div>
```

```
<div id="header">
<h1>Pendity Software</h1>
<h2>Style Guide</h2>
</div>
<div id="links">
<a href="guide.php">Guide</a>
<a href="suggestions.php">Suggestion Box
    </a>
<?php
if (isset($_SESSION['name'])) {
    echo '<a>Welcome, ', htmlspecialchars
        ($_SESSION['name']), '</a>';
} else {
    echo '<a href="login.php">Sign in</a>';
}
if (isAdmin($_SESSION['userid'])) {
?>
<p>Admin Only:</p>
<a href="users.php">User List</a>
<?php
}
?>
</div>
<div id="main">
```

Next, it's time to work on the suggestion box. The suggestion box will contain a link to make a new suggestion and will list any existing suggestions that are open for votes. The dates below use a concise format; you may choose another if you wish. We do want to be sure that only logged in users can make suggestions; we check $_SESSION['userid'] for this.

suggestions.php

```
<?php
session_start();
require 'connect.php';
require 'header.php';
?>
```

```
<h1>Suggestion Box</h1>
<?php
if (empty($_SESSION['userid'])) {
    echo '<p>Sign in to add a suggestion.</p>';
} else {
    echo '<p><a href="suggestion-new.php">
    New suggestion</a></p>';
}
$query = "SELECT *, DATE_FORMAT(date_proposed,
    '%b %e') AS date_proposed FROM suggestions
    WHERE status = 'Proposed' ORDER BY
    date_proposed";
$result = $db->query($query) or exit('Error
    retrieving suggestions.');
if ($result->num_rows) {
    echo '<table><tr><th>Category</th>
        <th>Summary</th><th>Proposed</th>
        </tr>';
    while ($row = $result->fetch_assoc()) {
    echo "<tr><td>$row[category]</td>",
    "<td><a href=\"suggestion-detail.php?
        sid=$row[sid]\">",htmlspecialchars(
        $row['summary']), "</a></td>",
    "<td>$row[date_proposed]</td></tr>";
    }
    echo '</table>';
} else {
    echo '<p>There are currently no proposed
        suggestions.</p>';
}
require 'footer.php';
```

Next, from much earlier, we have a file called *suggestion-new.html*.
It's time to flesh that out just a little bit, including adding the header and
adding a field for a summary of the suggestion. After adding the header,
the description (which needs to be renamed) seems a little tall; we've
trimmed it to 30 rows below:

suggestion-new.php

```php
<?php
require 'header.php';
?>
<p>Please add a suggestion for the Style Guide
    below.</p>
<form action="suggestion-save.php"
    method="post">
<p>Section:
<select name="section">
<option>General</option>
<option>HTML</option>
<option>CSS</option>
<option>PHP</option>
<option>SQL</option>
</select></p>
<p>Summary: <input type="text" name=
    "summary" maxlength="100"/></p>
<p>Description<br/><textarea name=
    "description" cols="80" rows="30">
    </textarea></p>
<p><input type="submit" name="submit"
    value="Save"/> <input type="submit"
    name="submit" value="Cancel"/></p>
<?php
require 'footer.php';
```

There are many ways to handle the *Cancel* button. We could check to see if it was pressed and redirect early. We could make the button not part of the form and take the user somewhere else directly. In the script below, we've opted to make sure the user pressed the *Save* button before saving, so pressing the *Cancel* button simply skips to the redirect. The summary and description fields are escaped, but we've forced the section to be one of the allowed values. Although there is a set list of options to choose from, it's possible to edit a form from using developer tools in the browser to send any data someone wants, and since we're building this for developers, perhaps there's someone on the team who thinks they're funny. Although switch performs a loose comparison, all data received via the form is string data, so we don't need to worry about comparing integer 0 with text strings.

suggestion-save.php

```php
<?php
session_start();
if ($_POST['submit'] === 'Save') {
    require 'connect.php';
    switch ($_POST['section']) {
    case 'HTML':
    case 'CSS':
    case 'PHP':
    case 'SQL':
        $section = $_POST['section'];
        break;
    default:
        $section = 'General';
    }
    $summary = $db->escape_string(
        $_POST['summary']);
    $description = $db->escape_string
        ($_POST['description']);
    $uid = $_SESSION['userid'];

    $query = "INSERT INTO suggestions
    (category, summary, description, status,
    uid)
    VALUES ('$section', '$summary',
        '$description', 'Proposed', $uid)";
    $db->query($query) or exit('An error
        occurred saving.');
}
header('Location: suggestions.php');
```

Next, we need the detail page. This should show all information about the suggestion. We'll probably also link to this same page from the style guide itself so people can see the details of each suggestion. This page can be planned to work in both cases. If the suggestion is still only proposed, there should be a way to vote on it and to show the votes. If the suggestion has been approved or rejected, we need only show the date that occurred. It should also show all comments, and if still in proposed state, allow additional comments. One possible way to accomplish all of this is in the script below. It references two images: *up.png* and *down.png*.

These are simply up and down arrows in PNG format. Feel free to make your own.

suggestion-detail.php

```php
<?php
session_start();
$sid = (int)$_GET['sid'];
var_dump($sid);
if ($sid == 0) {
    header('Location: index.php');
    exit();
}
require 'connect.php';
/* Although * selects all, naming a later field
    the same as a table column is okay.
    fetch_row() handles it fine. fetch_
        assoc() overwrites the first value with
        the later one,
    but that's okay; only the later field is
        used.
*/
$query = "SELECT *, DATE_FORMAT(date_
    proposed, '%c/%e/%y') AS date_proposed,
    DATE_FORMAT(date_voted, '%c/%e/%y') AS
    date_voted FROM suggestions INNER JOIN
    users USING (uid) WHERE sid = $sid";
$result = $db->query($query) or exit
    ('Error retrieving suggestion');
if ($result->num_rows == 0) {//not a valid ID
    header('Location: index.php');
    exit();
}
require 'header.php';
$row = $result->fetch_assoc();
$status = $row['status'];
echo "<h2>$row[category]</h2>",
    "<h3>", htmlspecialchars(
        $row['summary']), "</h3>",
```

```php
    "<p><b>$row[status]</b> on ";
if ($status == 'Proposed') {
echo $row['date_proposed'], ' by <i>',
    htmlspecialchars($row['firstname'].'
    '.$row['lastname']), '</i></p>';


$upclass = ''; $downclass = '';//These get
    used to change the color of the border for
    our vote
$query = "SELECT uid, vote, firstname,
    lastname FROM user_votes INNER JOIN users
    USING (uid) WHERE sid = $sid";
$result = $db->query($query) or exit
    ('Error in vote query.');
$ups = array(); $downs = array();
while ($voterow = $result->fetch_
    assoc()) {
if ($voterow['vote'] > 0) {
$ups[] = "$voterow[firstname]
    $voterow[lastname]";
if (isset($_SESSION['userid']) &&
    $voterow['uid'] == $_SESSION['userid']) {
$upclass = 'selected';
    }
    } else {
$downs[] = "$voterow[firstname]
    $voterow[lastname]";
if (isset($_SESSION['userid']) &&
    $voterow['uid'] == $_SESSION['userid']) {
    $downclass = 'selected';
    }
    }
    }
if (empty($_SESSION['userid'])) {
echo "<p><img src=\"up.png\" class=\"voteicon
    $upclass\"/> ",
htmlspecialchars(implode(', ', $ups)), '</p>',
"<p><img src=\"down.png\" class=\
    "voteicon $downclass\"/> ",
```

```
htmlspecialchars(implode(', ', $downs)), '</p>',
'<p><b>Sign in to vote or leave a comment.
    </b></p>';
    } else {
echo "<p><a href=\"vote.php?sid=
    $sid&vote=1\"><img src=\"up.png\" class=
    \"voteicon $upclass\"/></a> ",
htmlspecialchars(implode(', ', $ups)), '</p>',
"<p><a href=\"vote.php?sid=$sid&vote=
    0\"><img src=\"down.png\" class=\"voteicon
    $downclass\"/></a> ",
htmlspecialchars(implode(', ', $downs)), '</p>';
    }
} else {
    echo $row['date_voted'], '</p>';
}
if (strlen($row['description'])) {
    echo '<p>Description:</p>',
'<p style="border: solid 1px #ddd;
    padding: 0.75em;">', nl2br(htmlspecialchars
    ($row['description'])), '</p>';
}
$query = "SELECT firstname, lastname, DATE_
    FORMAT(cdate, '%c/%e/%y %h:%i %p') AS cdate,
    ctext FROM comments INNER JOIN users USING
    (uid) WHERE sid = $sid";
$result = $db->query($query);
if ($result->num_rows) {
    echo '<hr/>';
}
echo '<div id="commentlist" style="margin:
    4em">';
while ($row = $result->fetch_assoc()) {
    echo '<div class="comment">',
'<p><b>', htmlspecialchars(
    $row['firstname'].' '.$row['lastname']),
    '</b><br/><i>', $row['cdate'],
    '</i></p>',
```

```php
'<p>', nl2br(htmlspecialchars(
    $row['ctext'])), '</p>';
}
echo '</div>';
if ($status == 'Proposed' && !empty
    ($_SESSION['userid'])) {
    ?>
    <hr/>
<form action="comment-save.php" method=
    "post">
<input type="hidden" name="sid" value=
    "<?= $sid ?>"/>
<textarea name="comment" cols="60" rows=
    "10"></textarea>
<p><input type="submit" value="Add
    Comment"/></p>
    </form>
    <?php
}
require 'footer.php';
```

Three new styles were used in the script above. Add them to *style.css*:

```css
.comment {
    background-color: #ffd;
    border-top: #333 solid 1px;
    border-bottom: #333 solid 1px;
    padding-left: 1.5em;
    padding-right: 1em;
}
.voteicon {
    height: 2em;
    border: 2px solid white;
}
.selected {
    border-color: #777;
}
```

Now we need to handle the action that happens on this page. Clicking the arrows leads to *vote.php*. Adding a comment leads to *comment-save.php*. We'll handle the latter first.

```php
<?php
session_start();
require 'connect.php';
$sid = (int)$_POST['sid'];
$uid = $_SESSION['userid'];
$text = $db->escape_string(
    $_POST['comment']);
$query = "INSERT INTO comments (sid, uid,
    ctext) VALUES ($sid, $uid, '$text')";
$db->query($query) or exit('An error
    occurred saving your comment.'. $query);
header("Location: suggestion-detail.
    php?sid=$sid");
```

And now to handle the voting. Recall that 1 is a vote up, 0 is a vote down, and that if more than half the users vote a particular way, the suggestion is accepted or rejected.

vote.php

```php
<?php
session_start();
require 'connect.php';
$sid = (int)$_GET['sid'];
$uid = $_SESSION['userid'];
if ($_GET['vote'] == 1) {
    $vote = 1;
} else {
    $vote = 0;
}
$query = "INSERT INTO user_votes (uid, sid,
    vote) VALUES ($uid, $sid, $vote) ON
    DUPLICATE KEY UPDATE vote = $vote";
$db->query($query) or exit('There was an error
    saving your vote.');
```

```php
/* Get the total number of users */
$query = "SELECT COUNT(*) FROM users";
$result = $db->query($query) or exit('Error
    getting user total.');
$row = $result->fetch_row();
$users = $row[0];
/* Now find the total */
$query = "SELECT vote, COUNT(*) AS total FROM
    user_votes WHERE sid = $sid GROUP BY
    vote";
$result = $db->query($query) or exit('Error
    getting vote totals.');
$statuses = array('Rejected', 'Accepted');
while ($row = $result->fetch_assoc()) {
    if ($row['total']/$users > 0.5) {/* More
    than half of users voted this way */
    $status = $statuses[$row['vote']];
    $query = "UPDATE suggestions SET
    status = '$status', date_voted = CURRENT_
    TIMESTAMP WHERE sid = $sid";
    $db->query($query) or exit("Error changing
    suggestion to $status");
    }
}
header("Location: suggestion-detail.
    php?sid=$sid");
```

And lastly, the guide. List the accepted suggestions by category. Because this page runs nearly the same query five times, it uses a prepared statement to do so. Note the call to $stmt->store_result so that it's able to use $stmt->num_rows before iterating through the result set.

```php
<?php
session_start();
require 'connect.php';
require 'header.php';
?>
```

```php
<div style="width: 620px; margin-left: auto;
    margin-right: auto;">
<?php
$categories = array('General', 'HTML', 'CSS',
    'PHP', 'SQL');
$query = "SELECT sid, summary, DATE_FORMAT
    (date_voted, '%c/%e/%y') AS date_voted FROM
    suggestions WHERE status = 'Accepted' AND
    category = ?";
$stmt = $db->prepare($query) or exit('An error
    occurred preparing the statement.');
$stmt->bind_param('s', $category) or exit('An
    error occurred binding parameters.');
foreach ($categories as $category) {
$stmt->execute() or exit('An error
    occurred executing the statement.');
    $stmt->store_result();
    if ($stmt->num_rows) {
echo "<h2>$category</h2><table
    class=\"styletable\"><tr><th>Summary
    </th><th style=\"width: 100px\">Approved
    </th></tr>";
$stmt->bind_result($sid, $summary, $date)
    or exit('An error occurred binding the
    result');
    while ($stmt->fetch()) {
echo "<tr><td><a href=\"suggestion-
    detail.php?sid=$sid\">$summary</a></td>
    <td>$date</td></tr>\n";
    }
    echo "</table>";
    }
}
?>
</div>
<?php
require 'footer.php';
```

And that's it! We have a working site! Users can sign up, make suggestions, leave comments, vote, and browse the guide! If they're not logged in, they can't make suggestions, leave comments, or vote.

FURTHER READING

The PHP manual can be found online at http://php.net/manual/en/index.php. It contains a full function reference, language reference, and information about many PHP extensions. It is further enhanced with the addition of user notes, though pay attention to the score they receive.

Of particular interest should be functions that handle strings (http://php.net/manual/en/book.strings.php), functions that deal with arrays (http://php.net/manual/en/ref.array.php), the time zone-aware DateTime class (http://php.net/manual/en/class.datetime.php), and the mysqli extension (http://php.net/manual/en/book.mysqli.php).

https://stackoverflow.com is a useful site for coders of all stripes to ask questions about problems that trip them up.

For a book that spends nearly 800 pages purely on PHP, *PHP Cookbook* covers a much more extensive array of topics in much greater depth (www.amazon.com/dp/144936375X).

EXTENDING THE STYLE GUIDE

The project presented in this book contained only a small amount of functionality, just enough to illustrate key points and how the different pieces work together. As you learn more about them, consider revisiting the project and implementing the following:

1. As written, although it blocks users from seeing certain UI elements if they are not logged in, the scripts that handle these submissions don't check for this, which leads to error messages being output. How could they be changed to handle this case better?
2. Although users are able to login, they are not able to log out! Provide a logout page. (Hint: how do we check to see if they're logged in?)
3. Some users would like to include code snippets, blocks of code that appear preformatted, with a fixed width font, and possibly a border and different color background. The appearance is easily done in CSS. Given that any HTML entered is sanitized when we output it, what could be done to allow the users this functionality? (Hint: provide different tags they can use. Research the PHP string functions for how to detect and replace these tags. This one is not for the faint of heart!)
4. Rejected submissions are not shown. This might cause people to suggest the same thing more than once. How can you include these, and where would you put them?
5. At the moment, when someone leaves the system, their record is deleted. This could cause some issues with their votes. When a user is deleted, should their votes be deleted? Should you check to see if any proposed suggestions become accepted or rejected?
6. Once a suggestion is accepted or rejected, it's no longer possible to see who voted which way on it. What if this should be shown? How does this work when a user is deleted later?

About the Author

Bob Terrell has completed a Bachelor of Science degree at Wentworth Institute of Technology. While there, he completed a class project to automate the gift drive of a popular nonprofit organization in the Boston area. The website resulting from that project is still in use today and has helped find gifts for over 16,000 children. He was also invited to teach HTML and PHP as a guest teacher to a younger class as part of a database course to help expand the school's community involvement.

He currently works as a software developer at a small company north of Boston that creates DOT-compliant truck tracking and fleet management software for trucking and line haul companies, using the technologies outlined in this book. He has 14 years of experience in HTML, CSS, PHP, and MySQL languages.

INDEX

OTHER TITLES FROM OUR
COMPUTER SCIENCE COLLECTION

Lisa MacLean, *Editor*

- *Information System Research: Fundamentals of Scientific Research for the Consumer* by Matthew Taylor
- *SQL By Example* by John Russo

Momentum Press is one of the leading book publishers in the field of engineering, mathematics, health, and applied sciences. Momentum Press offers over 30 collections, including Aerospace, Biomedical, Civil, Environmental, Nanomaterials, Geotechnical, and many others.

Momentum Press is actively seeking collection editors as well as authors. For more information about becoming an MP author or collection editor, please visit http://www.momentumpress.net/contact

Announcing Digital Content Crafted by Librarians

Concise e-books business students need for classroom and research

Momentum Press offers digital content as authoritative treatments of advanced engineering topics by leaders in their field. Hosted on ebrary, MP provides practitioners, researchers, faculty, and students in engineering, science, and industry with innovative electronic content in sensors and controls engineering, advanced energy engineering, manufacturing, and materials science.

Momentum Press offers library-friendly terms:
- *perpetual access for a one-time fee*
- *no subscriptions or access fees required*
- *unlimited concurrent usage permitted*
- *downloadable PDFs provided*
- *free MARC records included*
- *free trials*

The **Momentum Press** digital library is very affordable, with no obligation to buy in future years.

For more information, please visit **www.momentumpress.net/library** or to set up a trial in the US, please contact **mpsales@globalepress.com**.

CPSIA information can be obtained
at www.ICGtesting.com
Printed in the USA
JSHW062240040822
28865JS00006B/169